CROSSING THE BRIDGE:

GROWING UP NORWEGIAN-AMERICAN IN DEPRESSION & WAR:1925-1946

Earl A. Reitan
Normal, Illinois 61761

Best wish to Norma Ashbrook.

Earl A. Reitan

Crossing The Bridge
Growing Up Norwegian-American
In Depression & War
1925 – 1946
by
Earl A. Reitan

© Earl A. Reitan 1999
ISBN 1-883477-28-X

Library of Congress
Catalog In Publication Number 98-89808

Published by
Lone Oak Press

To Clayton, Phil, and Norma,
who crossed the bridge with me

Contents

PREFACE

Purpose

This book tells the story of the life of my family and myself to 1946, when at the age of twenty-one, I was honorably discharged from the U. S. Army and began preparing for a career as an historian. My purpose goes beyond mere reminiscence. This memoir records the progress of three generations of a Norwegian-American family as they made their way across the bridge that led from the Old Country to the New World.

The first generation, my paternal grandparents, came to the United States from Trondheim, Norway, settled in Grove City, Minnesota, raised a large family, and became prominent citizens of that small town. They adopted the English language and American citizenship and participated in local government. My maternal grandparents were Danes who farmed nearby. The second generation, my parents, had to cope with the usual problems of assimilation aggravated by Depression and war. Growing up, I observed their struggle, and this memoir is presented from that perspective. My generation was the fortunate generation. We completed the crossing of the bridge and have enjoyed the opportunities offered by post-war America.

In the pursuit of their aspirations, my grandparents and parents were supported by their Norwegian-American culture and their Lutheran faith. They were strong people, who believed that the right thing to do was also the best thing to do. They allowed very little deviation from the straight and narrow path, but within those limits there was plenty of room for personal growth. They knew that survival required hard work and prudent management of money. They supported their ministers and churches, and they valued highly the opportunities provided by the public schools and church-supported colleges. I, my two brothers, my sister, and indeed our generation are the beneficiaries of their courage and character.

Photo - C.C. Reitan Family

Front - C.C., Carl, Karen, Middle - Earnest, Reuben
Back - Conrad, Beatrice, Gustav, Rose, Ludovic, Louise

The Name

We Reitans bear a distinctive name that few outside Norway or Norwegian-American circles can pronounce. My grandfather, C. C. Reitan came to Minnesota from Reitan Gaarden, near Trondheim, and this place is presumably the source of the name. The Norwegian pronunciation of the name is "Ray-tunn," with a rolled "r" and a rising inflection on the last syllable. In Grove City, Minnesota, my ancestral home, this pronunciation was corrupted to "Ritten." One Sunday my cousin Audrey, who was visiting Grandpa Reitan's farm, returned from Sunday school, where they had sung the hymn, "Will my Name be Written There?" "If it's Reitan (Ritten) here, it will certainly be Reitan there too," she stated indignantly.

4

I pronounced my name "Ritten" until I went to Concordia College in Moorhead, Minnesota. In that part of the state the name was pronounced "Rye-tahn," so I conformed to that pronunciation. When I moved to Illinois, however, I decided to pronounce the name as "Rye-tan," which was as close to phonetic as I could make it. Many people have difficulty giving equal stress to both syllables, and are inclined to put the accent on the second syllable.

It was in Oslo in 1970 that I heard the Norwegian pronunciation of my name. I went into a bank to cash a travelers check. The teller asked me to wait until my name was called.

I was sitting on a bench when I heard a musical Norwegian male voice call softly, "Ray-tunn?"

It had a lovely sound.

BEGINNING THE CROSSING:
THE FIRST GENERATION & THEIR FAMILIES
(TO 1925)

Grandpa and Grandma Reitan

My story and that of my family could begin like many an eighteenth-century novel: "My parents were poor but honorable and did their best to give me a good start in life, despite their humble circumstances." In the English novel the leading character usually comes from Shropshire, Devon, or some other rural shire. My equivalent was Meeker County, Minnesota, about eighty miles west of the Twin Cities, a gently rolling county of family farms and small towns, with Litchfield as the county seat. Both my parents were born in Meeker County, where I was also born, in 1925, in the pleasant little town of Grove City.

Christian Clement Reitan, my paternal grandfather, was born in 1849, the son of Clement and Anna Reitan. In 1870, at the age of twenty-one, he emigrated from Norway to Northfield, Minnesota, where he worked for a farmer for four years, learning the English language and Norwegian-American ways. Then he moved to Minneapolis, where he was employed by a fellow-countryman, A. C. Haugen, as a clerk in a grocery store for another four years. Apparently C. C. and his employer hit it off very well, for in 1877 C. C. returned to Norway and married Karen Kindseth, sister of Haugen's wife, who also had grown up in the vicinity of Trondheim. They had ten living children, seven boys and three girls. Another daughter died at birth.

Having paid his dues, learned the language, saved some money, and acquired a wife, C. C. was now ready to launch out on his own. In 1879 he returned to Minneapolis and renewed his

7

employment with Haugen for a year. He then moved to Grove City, six miles west of Litchfield, where Haugen staked him to enough capital to establish a grocery store. Three years later he paid off Haugen and owned his own store. The store was located in a plain frame building with wooden floors, a counter, and shelves along the walls.

C. C. was a townsman, not a farmer like so many Norwegian settlers, and he had an entrepreneurial spirit. Shortly after settling in Grove City, C. C. went into partnership with John Christensen to build a grain elevator of 50,000 bushels capacity, which they later sold to the Northwestern Elevator Company. In 1885 he travelled to Europe, visiting England, France, Belgium, Germany, Norway, and Sweden.

Christian Clement Reitan,   Grandma Albertina Jensen
Karen Kindseth Reitan

C. C. Reitan was regarded as one of the pillars of the Grove City community. He and Grandma Reitan were among the organizers of the Norwegian Lutheran church in Grove City. He was a justice of the peace, and for thirty-five years he was clerk of the school district. In 1893 C. C. Reitan's business failed and he turned to farming, living for the next twenty-two years on a farm near Grove City. Then he retired to the family house in Grove City. Perhaps C. C. Reitan was a victim of circumstances. The year 1893 was marked by a national financial panic that resulted in many bank failures and personal bankruptcies. Was my grandfather a casualty of American boom-bust capitalism, as my father was in 1929? Probably.

Grandpa stayed in touch with his bachelor brother, Ole C. Reitan, who was in business in Duluth. "Uncle O.C.," as he was called, assisted several of the children to get started in life. A letter written by Grandpa Reitan in 1909 indicates that three of his children (Conrad, Ludovic, Rose) were in Duluth at that time. Despite his evident interest in the family, Uncle O. C. never visited Grove City, except to attend his brother's funeral.

Despite his financial problems, C. C. Reitan eventually managed to provide a comfortable living for his family. Evidence of his prosperity may be seen in the splendid dining room set that he acquired. There was a long table, a magnificent buffet, and twelve chairs with red-plush seats. I have one of these chairs, which have been distributed among his grandchildren as heirlooms.

Photo (Top Left) - Jensen Girls - Front, Caren Helene, Hilda; Back, Mary, Minne Photo (Bottom) Albertina Jensen and Caren Helene knitting for the Red Cross during World War I

Grandma Reitan was a strong woman. For many years she was president of the Ladies' Aid Society of the Norwegian Lutheran

Church, the highest social position to which a Grove City woman could aspire in those days. She was strongly opposed to alcoholic beverages, and was a member of the Women's Christian Temperance Union (WCTU), the organization that lobbied successfully for Prohibition. She refused to live on the farm during the winter and insisted on having a house in town where her daughters could be properly raised and educated. My mother told me that she was in awe of Grandma Reitan as long as she lived.

Grandma Reitan died in 1926, the year after I was born. I still have a pair of little red mittens that she knitted for me. She apologized to my mother for the quality of the knitting; her eyes had gotten so dim and her fingers so stiff that she could not maintain her previous standards. She said she had ripped them out several times before deciding to finish them as best she could.

In Grandpa Reitan's generation, the Norwegian language was a vital part of the Grove City community and could be heard in church on Sunday and on street corners on Saturday nights. As time passed, English became the usual language of my grandparents, at home, at church, and elsewhere. Several of Grandpa Reitan's letters to my Aunt Rose (who spoke Norwegian fluently) have been preserved. They are well written, in correct and flowing English, which seems to have become his everyday language. In Grandpa Reitan's case (and probably Grandma's, too) the crossing of the bridge in terms of language was well advanced.

My grandparents' transition to American citizenship was made easier by being part of a large Norwegian-American community in a strongly Scandinavian state, where their moral and religious values were widely shared. The Norwegian Lutheran Church gave them a secure base for their personal and social life. This branch of Lutheranism was dominated by pietists who had rejected the Norwegian state church. They brought to America their strong emphasis on personal salvation, prayer, and strict morality. The Puritanism that underlay American culture in those days was congenial to this generation of Norwegian immigrants.

In terms of national identity, I believe that C. C. Reitan's American citizenship was more than a legal status. As a well-travelled man, he knew about different countries and their distinctive national characteristics. I have no doubt that when he left Norway for America, and then returned to bring back his bride, he had made a commitment to the United States that was complete, without looking back. When he was able to do so, he brought his parents to Grove City, and they are buried in the Reitan plot in the Norwegian Lutheran cemetery.

Grandpa Reitan was killed in 1918 when he, with many of the townspeople, gathered at the railroad tracks to welcome and chat with troops on a troop train bound for World War I. While this patriotic gathering was taking place, the fast train came rushing through on the main track. The crowd scattered, but C. C. was deaf and did not hear the train coming. He was hit by the train and killed.

Photo – Grove City,
C. C Reitan
Memorial Clock

C. C.'s untimely death while performing a patriotic act was probably one reason why a memorial clock bearing his name was placed in our church, although I am inclined to believe that the clock was also an expression of esteem for a respected citizen of the town. In my boyhood the clock was prominently displayed near the pulpit, bearing the legend: "In Memoriam: C. C. Reitan."

The clock was later moved to the back of the church. I was informed that the minister did not like having the clock behind the pulpit, because the congregation got restless if the sermon passed a certain time. The clock also informed some ladies that it was time to slip out quietly and go home to put the potatoes on for Sunday dinner.

Photo – Grove City, Immanuel Lutheran Church

Photo – Grove City, Reitan Gravestone

Some years ago I stumbled on another memorial to Grandpa Reitan. On a trip to New York City, my wife and I took a ferry to the Statue of Liberty, which then housed a museum of immigration. In the museum were half a dozen computer keyboards and monitors that provided access to photographs of immigrants.

On an impulse I punched R-E-I-T-A-N. Up came a familiar photograph of Grandpa and Grandma Reitan. The people standing around me were as astonished as I was to discover that my grandparents were immortalized in the Statue of Liberty. I learned later that one of my cousins had contributed the photograph in 1976 when the museum was opened as part of the Bicentennial of the Declaration of Independence.

The most meaningful symbolic representation of my grandparents stands in the Norwegian-Lutheran cemetery: a gray granite gravestone with the name "Reitan" in bold letters. It is noteworthy that C. C. and his wife did not put their names on the markers of their individual graves, which read simply: "Father," "Mother." They seem to have accepted that their role in life was to be parents and ancestors.

The cemetery was not far from our Grove City house. I recall walking with my father to the cemetery on a sunny Sunday afternoon. He pushed the lawn mower in front of him while I skipped on ahead. He would tell me about Grandpa as he tended the grave, cutting the grass and trimming the peonies. He always spoke happily and nostalgically about life on the Reitan farm. At an early age I sensed special tenderness as he pointed out the grave of his younger brother Reuben, but it was many years later that I learned the tragic story of Reuben's death.

Several years ago I placed a gravestone for Carol and myself on the Reitan plot where my parents are buried. Although I have wandered far from my Reitan forebears geographically and culturally, I wanted to have a stone someplace with my name on it. And the only proper place was the family plot purchased by C. C. Reitan for himself and his descendants a century or more ago.

The Reitans

My sense of family was strengthened by my Reitan uncles and aunts. Some remained in the vicinity of Grove City, and others who had moved away made occasional visits. Unlike my mother's side of the family, my Reitan uncles were not farmers. In those days business was the open door to success, and they took that route. Their aspirations (or perhaps their opportunities) did not extend to professional careers as a doctor, lawyer, or clergyman.

As I grew up it became apparent to me that Uncle Conrad, the eldest son and the most successful in worldly terms, was the most esteemed member of the family. Conrad was distinguished in appearance and confident in manner. He rarely returned to Grove City, and a visit from Conrad was indeed a notable event.

As was usual among immigrants, the family network was important to Uncle Conrad's advancement. Conrad was born in Grove City in 1879. He left the farm and went to Duluth, where he was assisted in getting started by Uncle O. C., who was already established in business. Conrad settled there and did well as a grain broker.

Photo – Reitans – Rose, Carl, Conrad, Louise,
Earnest, Gust, Beatrice

When I was about twelve, our family took a trip to Duluth to visit Uncle Conrad, Aunt Joy, and our Duluth cousins. They lived in a fine house on Lake Superior. I was awed by their soft upholstered furniture, thick carpeting, and a fireplace with hearth, screen, and andirons. Their handsome, lively children were older than us. They looked like the children I read about in books or saw in movies. My brothers and I were obviously shy country cousins. On that trip we also visited Uncle Lud and his family in nearby Ironwood, Michigan.

In the 1950s I drove Aunt Louise and Aunt Rose to Duluth to visit Conrad. Instead of the legendary Conrad of my boyhood memories, I found a sad old man living alone in a big old house. When Aunt Rose began speaking fondly of "Papa" and "Mama" and their happy life on the farm, Conrad exploded:

"He was an old fool," Conrad said. "He let his partner steal him blind, and then he took up farming – something he knew nothing about. Mother and us children slaved on that farm with nothing because he was an old fool! I couldn't wait to get out of there."

Aunt Rose was shocked speechless. Aunt Louise, who was second to Conrad in age, remained silent during this outburst.

Conrad and Louise were the oldest children; they remembered the difficult times. My father and Aunt Rose were younger children; they remembered when times were better. After Conrad died, his children sent his ashes to Aunt Rose. She took his ashes to the Reitan plot, accompanied by a Lutheran minister, and had them reverently interred. So he returned to his father and Grove City after all.

The second child in C. C.'s family, Aunt Louise, was a handsome, warm-hearted, gracious woman. Undoubtedly she, like Conrad, wanted desperately to get off the farm, and perhaps out of Grove City too. Although I can only speculate, this is probably the reason that she married a stern, rather fierce-looking dentist named Meudeking who worked for the federal Indian Service. The marriage broke up because Aunt Lou could not accept the frequent traveling required by his job. They remained on good personal terms and Aunt Lou continued to do his sewing and perform other wifely chores. Their elder daughter married and settled with her husband in the interior of Alaska, where they were pioneers. The younger daughter, Audrey (cited in the Preface), died in childhood.

I remember Aunt Lou in the 1930s, when she had become the emancipated divorcee, living in the Twin Cities. Occasionally she would visit us, sometimes with one of her boyfriends in tow. One of them I remember as a genial, good-looking fellow with sharp clothes and a flashy car. After the war, when I came to know Aunt Lou better, she was sadder but wiser.

Photo – Dad, Mom, Aunt Evelyn, Uncle Carl

About 1940 Aunt Lou took a job as housekeeper for a retired railroad conductor who lived in Winona, Minnesota. He repeatedly asked her to marry him and eventually she did, although this semi-dotard was far removed from the kind of man she used to run around with. When the conductor died Aunt Lou was left with his house and his railroad pension, which enabled her to get along. I don't think either of her marriages brought her much happiness.

Near the end of her life, Aunt Lou moved to a small apartment in Willmar. Her old age must have been lonely: occasionally she visited her daughter in Alaska, but it was a long and difficult trip. On my trips from Illinois to Minnesota I would sometimes visit Aunt Lou, and we became rather close.

I last saw Aunt Lou on her deathbed. Carol and I were driving back from a visit to my mother in Minnesota. I had been told that she was in the hospital in Willmar and was not expected to live. I stopped briefly to visit her. Since it was about 10 p.m., Carol stayed in the car with baby Julia while I ran into the hospital to find out if I could see her.

I asked the nurse on duty if I could see my Aunt Louise briefly.

"Don't wake her if she is asleep," I said.

"It doesn't matter," the nurse replied, softly.

The ward was dark and silent as I approached her bed.

I touched her gently and said: "Aunt Lou. It's me. Earl."

"Oh Earl, you came!", she replied, in a voice that was both pleased and plaintive.

She was dying.

I don't know what we said – probably not very much. Then I left. She died a few days later.

Aunt Beatrice was the "character" of the family. She was an earthy, good-natured, energetic woman with a loud laugh and great enthusiasm for life. Her appearance was shapeless and almost comical; she seemed to have decided early that she was not pretty and would dress accordingly. Aunt Beattie's first husband was a railroad man named Swanson, who died a few years after they were married. They lived in Willmar.

Her second marriage was to Maurice Nelson, a tall, strong man with rugged features, a deep voice, a warm smile, and a rich Swedish brogue, who loved to talk and laugh. Maurice had been interested in Beatrice before she married Swanson. When he learned that she had decided to marry his rival he remarked: "I'll have her yet!" He did, too. They were married after Swanson died, and they both lived to celebrate their fiftieth wedding anniversary.

In his youth, Uncle Maurice had been a cowboy in western North Dakota. He once told me how he and his comrades would come riding and whooping into town, firing their pistols in the air. He added that he did not want me to mention this part of his life to Aunt Beattie.

When I was a little boy, Uncle Maurice was the town constable in Grove City. I admired him enormously. One time we were eating Sunday dinner at their house. Someone noticed that I was struggling to cut and eat the skin of my chicken. When I was asked why I was eating the skin I replied: "So I can grow up big and strong like Uncle Maurice and be a policeman." Apparently I had noticed that Maurice ate the skin of his chicken. Maurice remembered and retold that story to the end of his days.

Another childhood incident tells something about me. I was eating a piece of chocolate cake. Uncle Maurice noticed that I was eating the cake but not the frosting.

"Don't you like frosting?" he asked.

"That's the best part," I replied, "that's why I save it for the last."

Uncle Maurice liked that idea, too.

For some years Beatrice and Maurice lived on a farm between Grove City and Atwater. They were noted for keeping an exceptionally clean barn. During the harvest large gangs of itinerant workers would ride the rails seeking employment. Uncle Maurice was one of the few farmers who would hire transient black workers, who were a rarity in our part of the country.

Aunt Rose was the Reitan who had the strongest sense of family, and some of her feeling (which my Dad shared) rubbed off on me. On our annual visits to Grove City we always stopped to see Aunt Rose in nearby Atwater, which my brothers and I called "Auntwater." She was an out-going, emotional woman with a great sense of humor and joy in life. She made us feel special, although maybe she was that way with everybody. As the youngest sister, Aunt Rose had been given a great deal of responsibility for looking after the three boys who brought up the rear of the family. That is probably the reason she was close to Dad.

As a young woman, Aunt Rose went off to school to become a teacher. She attended the Lutheran Normal School in Sioux Falls, South Dakota – an example of the network of institutions established by the immigrants to provide a comfortable transition for the next generation. In September, 1908, shortly after arriving at the normal school, she wrote to her father complaining of homesickness and headaches. The next term she stayed in Duluth with Uncle O. C. and attended the Minnesota state normal school there. She qualified to teach in rural schools, but I am not aware that she ever received a degree. She taught in a rural school south of Atwater for about four years. In those days, instruction was mainly in Norwegian, although English was used also.

Aunt Rose was married to Uncle Ben, a tall, strong man who farmed south of Atwater and later worked in the local feed mill. Uncle Ben seldom said much, but Rose was talkative enough for both of them. They had a modest house in Atwater, and when I knew them they did not own a car. They were active in the church and sang in the choir and in quartets. Aunt Rose was a prolific writer of letters, including an annual letter to me on my birthday. Every visit to Atwater included hearing letters from other members of the family. A letter from Conrad was a special treat.

Aunt Rose had a gorgeous singing voice and often sang at weddings and funerals. Her emotional nature was fully expressed in her singing. When my sister Norma was baptized in 1936, Aunt Rose came to our church to sing at the baptism. She sang a baptism hymn to the tune of *From Greenland's Icy Mountains*. The members of the congregation were astounded: they had never heard anything like it.

In my college days, when I was playing the violin, I had my violin along on one visit to her house. I played for her Ole Bull's *Saeterjentens Sondag*, probably pretty mechanically.

"You need to put more feeling into it," she said. "Like this."

Then she opened up with her big voice and sang with a combination of power and tenderness that I have never forgotten. I felt embarrassed at my feeble effort.

When Carol and I were married, Aunt Rose did not send a present. Several years later we stopped to visit her on one of our annual trips to Minnesota. At that time she gave us an ornate serving fork from the Reitan family silver. Undoubtedly she prized it very much. With some embarrassment she explained that she had meant to send the fork when we were married, but several of her nephews had been divorced and her gift always went with the wife. She added that she thought we had now been married long enough to be a safe bet. I resolved that if the worst happened I would keep faith with Aunt Rose by insisting on getting the fork. We are still married and we use the fork on special occasions.

My account of my Reitan relatives must include the skeleton in the family closet. While in high school my Dad's younger brother, Reuben, fell in love with a classmate named Florence Nelson. For whatever reason, Grandpa and Grandma Reitan ordered Reuben to have nothing to do with Florence. Reuben continued seeing Florence secretly and she became pregnant. When this circumstance was revealed, Grandpa and Grandma were furious that Reuben had committed this sin against God and had shamed the entire family. They shipped Reuben off to Uncle Conrad, who was by then established in Duluth.

At such a time, Grandpa Reitan fell back upon his Christian faith. I have a copy of a loving and emotional letter written by Grandpa to Reuben, in which he calls upon his erring son to repent:

"Oh, child," he writes, "hast thou fallen? Arise, and go with childlike Trust to thy Father, like the prodigal son, and humbly say, with heart and mouth, 'Father, I have sinned against heaven and before thee, and I am no more worthy to be called thy son.'" The letter continues with the assurance of forgiveness from both the heavenly and the earthly father.

In the purest Lutheranism, C. C. assures his errant son that salvation "does not originate in man, but is of God; it is not of man's willing but of God's mercy; it is not of man's work, it is the gift of God." At the bottom of the letter he added a verse from a hymn:

Oh my God, my Father!
Hear and help me to believe;
Weak and weary I draw near;
Thy child O God receive.
I so oft have gone astray;
To the perfect Guide I flee;
Thou will turn me not away,
Thy love is pledged to me.

In Duluth Reuben shot himself; his body was brought back to Grove City for burial. I can only conjecture the agony and shock of the Reitan family. When I was growing up this disaster was treated as a closely-held secret and was never mentioned, although probably everybody in Grove City knew what had happened. I was middle-aged when my mother told me about it. Then I understood the special tenderness that Dad showed when caring for Reuben's grave.

As to Florence Nelson, my well-meaning Uncle Gust (an older brother) married her to make an honest woman of her. Reuben's child was raised in Grove City by Florence's parents with the name Roger Nelson. One time in Grove City Mom pointed him out to me and said: "Earl, that boy is your cousin." I was surprised to learn that I had a cousin that I had not met. I recall the incident because Mom had a mysterious look in her eyes when she told me. Roger grew up to be a fine-looking young man who was killed in World War II.

Uncle Gust was for many years janitor of the school, where he was popular with the children for his kindness and good-natured jokes. Uncle Gust was an easy-going man, and he needed to be. They had a modest income and eight children in a small house. Dad and Uncle Gust were very friendly. We always visited Florence and Gust when we returned to Grove City for Dad's summer vacation. Aunt Florence was an unhappy woman known in Grove City for her sharp tongue. She appreciated our visits, and complained that the other Reitans did not treat her properly. Eventually she mellowed into a sweet little old lady, and my brothers and I continued to visit her until her death at an advanced age.

The baby of the Reitan family was my Uncle Carl, who was tall, slim, debonair, and loaded with charm. About the time of World War I, Dad went off to western North Dakota to begin a career in banking. Later, Carl joined him, and both Reitan boys were living there when Grandpa Reitan died in 1918. Later Dad and Uncle Carl returned to Minnesota: Dad to a bank in Grove City and Carl to a bank in New London, a small town in the next county.

They continued to maintain a close relationship. Carl and Dad were close in age and shared a common experience in banking. My mother, who was a very modest person, "got a kick" out of Carl, who was a sharp dresser and always looked really "swell." She also enjoyed Aunt Evelyn, Uncle Carl's wife, who was lively and talkative. In 1939 Uncle Carl, who drove high-powered cars at high speed on narrow roads, was killed in an auto accident. Surprisingly, I don't remember much about his funeral, although his death must have hit my parents hard.

When that generation of Reitans came of age, most of the trappings of Norwegian ethnicity had fallen by the wayside. Norwegian history, foods, songs, and stories were trotted out only for special occasions. I never heard my father speak Norwegian or even attempt it, except in some stock phrases. I once heard Aunt Beatrice jabbering on the telephone with one of her cronies in a comical jumble of colloquial Norwegian and recognizable English words. When I asked her if she was talking English or Norwegian she laughed and replied: "Norwegian, English – We just mix 'em up. They're all the same to us!"

Probably the most important and lasting aspect of the Norwegian inheritance was in the form of moral and social standards, preserved and disseminated by the Lutheran Church and taught within the family by precept and example, reinforced by the occasional stern rebuke. The Norwegian-American community of the 1920s and 1930s was parochial and conservative, but for that very reason it provided an unthreatening context within which the process of Americanization could take place. All that was needed to enter the American mainstream was advanced education, and that became the role of my generation.

The last time that I saw my Reitan uncles and aunts together was at Dad's funeral in January 1950. After the ceremony and interment, we gathered at Aunt Rose's house in Atwater. Present were Conrad, Lud, Gust, Louise, Beatrice, and Rose. The three youngest – Earnest, Reuben and Carl – were dead. It was evident that my Reitan uncles and aunts genuinely liked and respected each other. Being part of this gathering of Reitans was very important to me at a time of uncertainty and loss.

Earnest Reitan

My father, Earnest Adolph Reitan, I will characterize as a "Bob Cratchit": a likable, hard-working small town banker and a good family man, who managed to get himself off the farm but who struggled all his life to stay afloat. The tale that I shall tell gives much attention to the vicissitudes that he experienced in seeking to fulfill his responsibilities.

Wedding – Earnest A. Reitan, Caren Helene Reitan

The chronology of Dad's early life, as I know it, is skimpy. He was born in 1892, and he spent most of his early years on the farm. He seems to have been "Daddy's boy." He told me stories of how he would stay on the farm during the winter with Grandpa, helping with the chores and living mainly on sour cream and bread. The older children got off the farm as soon as possible, and Reuben and Carl lived in town during the winter with their mother and sisters. But Dad stayed on the farm into his twenties, and it was thought that he would take over the farm when Grandpa died.

By living on the farm, Dad missed much of his schooling during the winter months. Grandpa Reitan cut his hair, my Dad recalled, but not very well. In school, the other boys teased him and called him "Sheephead" due to his haircut. No wonder he preferred to stay home on the farm. To my knowledge, he was the only child in the family who did not graduate from Grove City High School. If asked, they probably would have voted him "least likely to succeed."

Dad's meager education was supplemented by attending Willmar Seminary, an academy sponsored by the Norwegian Lutheran Church. The purpose of the institution was to educate and acculturate immigrants and prepare some of them to go to college.

At that time Aunt Beatrice was married to Swanson and living in Willmar. Dad stayed with them. On Monday mornings he would get on the train in Grove City, laden with milk, cream, eggs, vegetables, and other farm produce which he brought to Beatrice to pay for his room and board. On Friday he returned on the train to Grove City with his empty buckets and baskets. How long this went on, I do not know. This phase of his education probably took place when he was in his late teens or early twenties.

Some time prior to Grandpa Reitan's death, Dad attended business college in Mankato. Probably he was there just for a few months to learn the rudiments of bookkeeping and business law. This was the sum total of Dad's formal schooling. His rudimentary education did little to expand his vocabulary, stimulate his mind, or broaden his imagination. I never saw him read anything more challenging than a newspaper. Through all the ups and downs of his adult life he subscribed to the Minneapolis *Journal*, which evidently had become part of his roots.

As a banker in small-town Minnesota and North Dakota, Dad was careful and meticulous. He understood farming and small-town businessmen, and that was all he needed to know. His handwriting was small and precise – a book-keeper's hand. He typed "hunt and peck," using the first two fingers of each hand. He could type rapidly using this system, although he made many errors. He developed an elaborate, flowing signature which, he said, a banker needed to prevent someone from forging his name. The signature began with a tall, swooping letter E, which flowed into the letter A, one side of which doubled as the beginning of a swooping R, followed by little squiggles that represented the rest of the name, ending with another swoop which crossed the T.

Dad got most of his education in "the School of Hard Knocks," which administered many blows in his lifetime. His first job was in a small bank at Voltaire, North Dakota, near Minot. He told me that he arrived in Voltaire in the afternoon and met his boss shortly before closing. His boss pulled down the shade in the window of the front door, announced that it was closing time, and told Dad to balance the books. When Dad asked his boss to show him where things were and how he wanted the job done the reply was: "Hell, No! That's your job." Dad was up until midnight doing the books, but he made it and his career in small-town banking was launched.

The bank in Voltaire was one of three little banks spread over a distance of about thirty miles. Dad and his boss would open one bank for a few hours. Then they would race through the dust (or mud, or snow, as the case might be) in a Model T Ford to the next town, where the bank would be open for a few hours. Next they would proceed to the third bank. After that they drove home and repeated the process the next day. Their daily trips across North Dakota were not that far removed from the days of the Wells Fargo stage coach. Judging from Uncle Maurice's tale of life in the Wild West, they probably found it prudent to pack a weapon and be ready to use it. It is likely that they carried a shotgun too, to bag an unwary pheasant.

Grandpa Reitan's obituary shows that in 1918 Dad was working in the bank in Voltaire. Uncle Carl was in the bank in Velva, another of the three related banks. It is likely that Dad was the first to go to North Dakota, and then he recommended Carl when a job opened up at Velva. Presumably the two young men lived together, or at least provided company for each other.

Some years ago I saw a TV program about the life of Eric Sevareid, the distinguished journalist and TV commentator. He grew up in Voltaire, North Dakota, where his father was the banker! The program showed scenes of the countryside around Voltaire, which is quite hilly, and pictures of the Sevareid family and friends. Since those pictures were taken about the time that Dad was working in Voltaire, it is probable that Eric Sevareid's father was Dad's boss.

When Grandpa Reitan died the question arose of what to do with the farm. Since the older sons had long since left the farm, there may have been some consideration of the idea that Dad would take it over. I don't think anyone thought for a moment that Carl would be a farmer.

Obviously Dad did not accept the opportunity, which would have made me and my brothers farm boys. The Reitans were really townspeople at heart, and Dad wanted to have a town job too. In later years he would talk longingly of farming eighty acres – a sure recipe for starvation. I think that kind of talk was nothing more than nostalgia at times of discouragement, and perhaps a desire to follow Grandpa Reitan's retreat from the business world to the farm. Nothing came of it.

I do not know how long Dad worked in North Dakota or when he came back to Minnesota, but when he was married in 1924 he was employed at the Merchants and Farmers State Bank in Grove City. His employer was Aaron Liedholm, about whom I know nothing. At my mother's funeral I met Liedholm's daughter, who told me that Dad was a popular figure in the bank and around town. There is no doubt in my mind that Dad was happy to be in his home town with his family and friends.

We moved away from Grove City in 1931, when I was six, but Dad and Mom maintained close ties with Grove City and Meeker County, where most of their relatives lived. Dad's vacations were usually spent visiting the old home town. When we left Grove City he lost his roots, and the rest of his life was a struggle to put down new ones.

Grove City: Our House

Grove City:
Merchants & Farmers
State Bank

The Jensens

Dad undoubtedly knew my mother's family, the Jensens, before he left for North Dakota, but he probably had had little direct association with them. The Jensens worshipped at Arndahl, a rural church. The children walked to a one-room rural school at nearby Rosendale, a country crossroads with a store and creamery. Caren Helene Jensen, my mother, was a shy farm girl eleven years younger than Dad. Furthermore, the Jensens were Danes, and in the pecking order of that time and place, Danes ranked below Norwegians.

I know almost nothing about my maternal grandfather, Jorgen Jensen. No photograph of him exists, since he would never permit his picture to be taken. He died in 1918 of a stroke. Mother described her father as a strong-willed, at times violent man. There was a reason for his bad temper. He had broken an arm which was never properly set, the bone knitting only partially. He wore a leather brace on his arm while doing farm work, and he suffered pain the rest of his life. As a girl, Mother was often called upon to rub his arm after he had put in a hard day's work in the field.

Unlike her husband, Grandma Jensen was a sociable, kindly soul. I recall her bustling around Grove City, doing her little errands and talking to anyone who would listen, sometimes to the extent of being a nuisance. In my boyhood we always stayed at her house when we returned to Grove City for Dad's summer vacation. At one time she lived in a house near the town pasture. It seems amazing that Grove City had a town pasture, but it must be remembered that these people grew up with animals and were accustomed to providing their own milk and eggs.

Later Grandma Jensen moved to a house almost directly across from our former Grove City home. This house had a shed in the back where she kept chickens. Grove City had many apple trees, and the tree in Grandma Jensen's yard always had abundant fruit in the late summer. Uncle Gust and Aunt Florence and their brood lived across the alley in back of Grandma Jensen's house, so we had kids to play with when we visited.

I do not know when Grandma Jensen left the farm. The eldest Jensen, my Uncle Christ, took over the farm and spent the rest of his life on the land where he was born. My guess is that Grandma moved to town when Christ was married, and since his children were the same age as me and my brothers, I would put the date at about 1924. We have pictures of Grandma Jensen on the farm when my brothers and I were small boys, and it is likely that she helped out on the farm in the summer.

Grandma Jensen had two children, Albert and Minnie Kring, by a previous marriage. Albert and his family remained in the area, but we rarely saw them. Minnie married and moved to Williston, North Dakota. Minnie was the natural leader of the family, and my mother liked her very much. As the wife of Jorgen Jensen, Grandma Jensen gave birth to Christ, Martin, Art, Emmanuel, Carl, Mary, Caren Helene (my mother), and Hilda.

The tasks on the farm were performed with human and horse power, and they were endless. From their earliest years all the children had to work. My Mother once told me: "We didn't go out to play, as you boys did. We always had to be doing something. That's just the way it was."

The boys did field work and the girls helped in the house and the barn. The chores connected with the cows, hogs, and chickens had to be done every day. One of the memorable events in my Mother's childhood was when they got a cream separator. Before that they had to skim the cream off the milk by hand. The tasks of cooking, washing, ironing, sewing, and mending were endless. As soon as they were old enough to leave home, the children had to get jobs, to bring in money and relieve the pressure on the household. The boys began as farm hands and the girls looked for jobs in domestic service. In the winter, however, some of these jobs disappeared, and then the house was crowded with young adults.

The Jensens were crowded in their modest farmhouse, which was Uncle Christ's and Aunt Vera's house when I knew it. One bedroom upstairs had three beds for the six boys, and another bedroom had two beds for the four girls. Mother recalled that, as a little girl, she enjoyed lighting the lamps, especially in the winter, when it got dark early. In my mind's eye I can imagine her in her early teens, quiet but smart, with braided hair, a long dress, hightop shoes, and an ironed apron, moving quickly and deftly to perform a household task that added a touch of gentility to a life that was demanding and sometimes harsh.

As the winter darkness fell, the younger girls would set the table while Grandma Jensen and the older girls cooked food on the cast-iron range, often fuelled with corn cobs. Everything would be in readiness for the moment when Jorgen Jensen and the boys, milking and other chores finished, came in from the barn, hanging up coats and caps, stamping the snow off their boots, washing up, and then sitting down for supper at the big table in the kitchen. Without radio or television, after supper the family would crowd into the small living room for reading, cards, or music, or find quieter spots upstairs in bedrooms crowded with beds. Everyone went to bed early.

The Jensens were musical, and music helped fill those long winter evenings. Helene and Hilda played the piano (the family could afford one somehow). I still have some of Mother's sheet music from the 1920s and earlier. Uncle Christ, the eldest, would call square dances; Mother recalled with amusement one time when he got mixed up and had the dancers colliding with each other. Uncle Carl played the accordion and Uncle Emmanuel the banjo. The Jensen brothers often played for parties and dances. Saturday night at the dance hall was welcome relief from their rigid regimen during the week.

I remember a summer Sunday afternoon at Grandma Jensen's house in Grove City. Several of the Jensens had gathered for Sunday dinner. A ferocious hail storm erupted. Mother rushed to the piano and began playing "Hail, Hail, the Gang's all Here." Everyone joined the singing.

When I left home I stayed in touch with Uncle Christ and Aunt Vera. Mother liked to visit them on the farm, and when I returned to Minnesota on my periodic visits I would take her there. Uncle Art and Aunt Emma lived on a farm nearby. When I was a boy I saw my Uncle Martin from time to time. He was a big, strong, friendly fellow who never married. He drove a little Willys car, the predecessor of the Jeep. Uncle Martin moved to North Dakota and I never saw him after that. He was a wheat farmer, apparently with considerable success. When he died he left a substantial estate that was divided among his brothers and sisters. My Mother received a legacy that she used to buy some needed new furniture.

Aunt Mary did not marry, although she would have been a terrific farm wife and mother. Her father's favorite, Mary was the only one who went to high school. For three summers I spent a few weeks on a farm where she was employed as the housekeeper. She became almost a second mother to me. The amount of work she did was enormous. For most of her life she supported herself as a cook in restaurants in Litchfield.

Aunt Hilda was especially close to Mother. Hilda was "Central" in the Grove City telephone system. Her office was located above the bank where Dad worked. I enjoyed visiting her office, watching her connect callers through her switchboard. Unfortunately, Aunt Hilda contracted tuberculosis and slowly wasted away. My last memory of her is of a pale skeleton, with large brown eyes and a translucent skin, lying on a bed in a sanitarium in northern Minnesota.

Special mention must be made of Uncle Emmanuel, the banjo player. Emmanuel and Martha, his wife, went to California during World War II where they worked in war plants and saved enough money to come back and buy the store at Rosendale. When they retired Emmanuel and Martha moved to Litchfield. They were warm-hearted people who gave considerable attention to Mother during her declining years in a nursing home there. At an advanced age, Uncle Emmanuel worked every summer at Green Lake Bible Camp, fixing boats and other equipment and serving as helper and friend to the children.

Helene Jensen

In her childhood photographs, my Mother always appears as a shy little girl. Eventually she blossomed into a lively, talkative, confident woman. The extent of her education was eight grades at the one-room Rosendale rural school. As she came of age, Helene Jensen had no opportunity for formal education or training. Like many farm girls she went into domestic service. She became a maid in Litchfield at the house of a doctor, appropriately named Dr. Cutts. Mrs. Dr. Cutts, as she was called, was English and considered herself the social leader of Litchfield. They had a large house and entertained frequently.

Working for Mrs. Dr. Cutts was a kind of education for Mother, at least in the social graces. At times she would cite Mrs.

Cutts as her authority for setting the table in a certain way or some other social convention. As a girl Mother was demure, quiet, and eager to please. She must have been the ideal housemaid.

When she had her own family, Mom was interested in new ideas about home-making and child-raising. She subscribed to *McCall's* magazine, at that time the leading periodical for married women. She could not afford the high fashion clothes depicted in the magazine, but perhaps *McCall's* had some influence as the fashions trickled down to mass-produced clothing and patterns. From time to time Mom tried new recipes, without much success at home, because the rest of us wanted to eat what we usually ate. When she entertained, however, she made attractive and different things to serve.

Mother left Mrs. Cutts to work in the bakery at the Litchfield Hospital. One of her memories was of a time when a fire broke out in the bakery and she responded quickly and effectively to put it out. At that moment she was a heroine in her small world. She was always interested in health care; in my opinion, her true calling was that of a nurse. However, she lacked the money and opportunity to go into nurse's training, so she followed the expected route: she got married, settled down, and had four children.

As I remember Mother during my boyhood, she was talkative with friends and relatives and always ready for any social event. She played bridge (the genteel game) while my Dad played only whist, and that very badly. She was Puritanical in her morality (as were most Lutherans), but she could modify it by sympathy when the code pinched too hard. She was an ardent supporter of Prohibition. My oldest political memory is of Mother sitting by the radio, weeping, when Roosevelt, the Democrats, and beer took over in March, 1933.

Like many women in that semi-frontier society, Mother was the civilizing force in our family. She saw to it that we were prompt, neatly dressed, and respectful of others. She would not tolerate bad language or angry quarrels. She admired educated people, such as ministers and school teachers. The fact that we became a family of educators is directly attributable to her. She taught us songs and games, and read Bible stories at bed-time. When we made our usual Saturday shopping trip to the county seat, a visit to the library to check out books was always included. She did her best to see that we got music lessons. Regular churchgoing was assumed in our family, although both parents deserve credit for that.

When I was a boy I had on my wall a water-color motto that Mother had made in school. It read: "Let every dawn of morning be to you as the beginning of life. Ruskin." This motto has remained in my mind throughout my lifetime, and it has often encouraged me when the upcoming day did not look promising. It becomes even more poignant as my life draws to its close.

Earnest and Helene

Some time after he returned to Grove City from North Dakota, Earnest Reitan began courting the shy little Danish girl. Mother told me that at first her family felt uncomfortable about Earnest's interest. The Reitans were town-dwellers and one of the prominent families of Grove City, while the Jensens were Danes and country people. Then there was the skeleton in the Reitan closet – the affair of Reuben, of which her older brothers and sisters were aware. When she began "walking out" with Earnest Reitan, they reminded her that she was treading on dangerous ground.

At any rate, my mother and father were married in September 1924. Mother's wedding dress was simple and her jewelry modest; once when I showed her wedding picture to her she described herself as a girl who liked to be "very plain." For reasons unknown to me, Aunt Rose arranged the wedding, which took place at the Norwegian Lutheran Church in Atwater, not in Immanuel Lutheran in Grove City or at Arndahl. Why? Both mothers were elderly widows, and perhaps neither felt able to undertake a wedding. Possibly, both families disapproved of the union. Under the circumstances, it was natural for Dad to call on Aunt Rose, who had been something of a mother to the younger boys. When I was a boy we had a tiny blue glass slipper that read: "Fergus Falls, Minnesota." Mom kept toothpicks in it. It is my recollection that it was a souvenir of their wedding trip.

As to their marriage, what child ever really knows anything about how its parents got along? In those days people married for life and each partner had clearly defined responsibilities. Dad made a scanty living but we were always respectable. Mother worked in the house and raised four children. As far as I could tell, neither dominated the other, or even attempted it. Differences were not aired at the dinner table or at any other place where the children were present. I am not aware of any violent quarrels between them: shouting, nagging, or snippy comments were not part of our life. Both were fair-minded and reasonable, and decisions were made on that basis.

Nor did they display overt signs of love and tenderness either. We were a tightly knit family, but we did not indulge in physical expressions of affection: we were not kissers and huggers. Looking back, it seems to me that Dad and Mom got along well enough. Unknown to them, I overheard one important private conversation which will be revealed in its proper place. In that conversation they were open and supportive.

The family was the center of my parents' lives; they took the children with them in almost everything they did. They worked hard and watched their pennies, but they found time for pleasant but inexpensive family activities too. Our life was narrow and rigid, but it gave us respect in the tiny communities where we lived, provided a moral base that enabled us to survive tough times, and gave the children a set of aspirations that eventually bore fruit.

Uncle Emmanuel was present at Mother's funeral in 1994, the only remaining Jensen of her generation. The widows of Christ, Art, and Carl were present. At the funeral, I saw some of my Jensen cousins for the first time in many years. They are fine, upstanding people, as one would expect. When I was growing up I saw my Jensen relatives as much as the Reitans, but I did not identify with them. Considering Mother's influence on our family, I now think that perhaps the Jensen streak in me was more important than I realized.

Nevertheless, I always knew that I was a Reitan, not a Jensen. I look, talk, smile, and walk like my father. When I was a little boy, people often commented that I looked like Earnest. I always felt good about that. Sometimes when I sit in an easy chair, legs crossed and hands folded, I have a startling recollection that Dad sat just that way. Mother's influence on my life will be apparent as this memoir unfolds, but my personal identification has always been with the Reitan side of my family. Why? I do not know.

THE SECOND GENERATION HITS A SNAG (1925-1935)

Grove City

It was my good fortune to be born into the real-life equivalent of Garrison Keillor's fictional "Lake Wobegone." With a population of about 200, Grove City was identified by its distinctive water tower (now replaced), which could be spotted from a considerable distance as it rose up through the trees. The town had been laid out along the main line of the Great Northern Railroad. The famous *Empire Builder*, coming from the Twin Cities on its way to Fargo and the West Coast, flashed through the town but did not stop. The main business street was also U.S. 12, a concrete highway parallel to the tracks. Most of the houses were built south of the highway and tracks, where the land sloped gently upward toward the school and the Norwegian Lutheran church.

The people were a homogeneous population of hard-working, responsible Scandinavian-Americans, who lived in well-kept frame houses along tree-lined streets. Most of them had been born in the United States. A few immigrant settlers remained, and some still talked longingly about "the Old Country." One old-timer returned to Norway to live out his last years in his birthplace. After a few months he returned to Grove City: "'tings yust veren't da saeme," he said.

Grove City served the surrounding countryside with a business district about two blocks long, including two banks (Grove City State Bank, Merchants and Farmers State Bank), two or three grocery stores, a furniture store, several grain elevators, a creamery, gas station, garage, farm implement dealer, and several other small businesses. The stores were open on Saturday nights when the farmers came to town to do their shopping and see their friends. In the summer the merchants offered free movies (silent, of course), shown outdoors on the side of a building. The people sat on discarded church pews while they watched the movie, conversed, or ate two-scoop ice cream cones for a nickel.

This typical Midwestern small town was surrounded by beautiful, rolling southern Minnesota farmland. Agriculture was based on a stable, labor intensive form of dairy and mixed farming, the only kind of farming those immigrants knew. In the country were little crossroads places with a store and creamery which had such names as Acton, Rosendale, and Stroud. The county seat was Litchfield, six miles east on U.S. 12. Litchfield had the full range of small town businesses, including a movie theater and a weekly newspaper.

My Birth

The events surrounding my birth were unusual. On Sunday morning, May 3, 1925, Ella Redin, the local midwife, was called to the home of Uncle Gust and Aunt Florence, where she delivered twins, June and Jean. She had just finished that task and was relaxing for a few minutes when she was called to our house to deliver me. Grandma Reitan got three grandchildren on the same day.

In the spring of 1991 I stopped in Litchfield to visit Mother, who was in a nursing home there. I learned that Ella Redin, then ninety-six years old, lived in the same nursing home. I had a vague recollection of Ella Redin, for Mom and Dad used to see her when they visited Grove City.

In the nursing home I asked for Ella Redin and was directed to the corridor where she lived. As I entered the lounge I saw a nicely dressed little old lady sitting in a wheel chair. I immediately recognized the dark, lustrous eyes and the prominent nose, which I recalled from my boyhood days.

"Ella," I said, taking her hand, "I am Earl Reitan (Ritten). You brought me into this world."

"I know," she replied softly, "it was a Sunday."

How many people who are sixty-six years of age will meet the person who delivered them? And discover that the event is remembered to the day?

What were the thoughts and feelings of Earnest Reitan on May 3, 1925? I think I can answer that question. After I had left home he wrote me an annual birthday letter. It always began something like this: "X years ago today was a Sunday, and I was the proudest and happiest man in the world."

Why not? On May 3, 1925 Earnest Reitan was thirty-three years of age. After many vicissitudes he held a job that he liked in a business which seemed secure; he lived in his hometown surrounded by the family and friends whom he had known all his life; he owned a little yellow house; and inside the little yellow house was a pretty wife and a newborn baby.

What else did Earnest Reitan want out of life?

In May 1957, I was thirty-two years of age. Our daughter, Julia, had been born a few weeks earlier. To accommodate a family of three we bought a little yellow house in Normal, Illinois. When we moved into the house I had a job that I liked in the career for which I had spent years of preparation. I had good friends and colleagues, and I lived in a pleasant small town. Inside my little yellow house were a pretty wife and a three-week old baby.

That evening, when the moving day activities were finished, I stepped out of the house into the back yard to get a breath of fresh air. Underfoot was the first piece of land that I had ever owned. Overhead a nearly full moon was shining; a warm, soft spring breeze caressed my face and rustled through the trees. I was so proud and happy. My heart swelled to such an extent that I had difficulty breathing. The mist which covered my eyes blurred the pale moon.

Did Earnest Reitan step into his back yard for a breath of fresh air on Sunday evening, May 3, 1925?

He probably did.

How did he feel?

I think I know.

The Church

The Church taught me that I was an important individual in the eyes of God and my family, and a member of a caring community. Most of the Norwegian immigrants to Minnesota were from the pietist branch of Norwegian Lutheranism. Theirs was a tender-minded, warm-hearted Christianity. The liturgy was simple and dignified, and sung by the pastor and the congregation. The service included readings from the King James Bible, graceful collects (formal prayers), singable hymns, among which were many English and American favorites, and a Gospel message from the pulpit. Lutheran morality was narrow, but it was less a matter of dogmatic pronouncements or fear of hellfire than a pragmatic adjustment to survival in an unforgiving land.

In its modest good taste, Immanuel Lutheran Church was a fine example of Norwegian immigrant architecture: a white frame building with a graceful spire, a white altar rail with dark red cushions, and a white altar topped by a painting of Christ in Gethsemane. In the back was a small balcony. The memorial clock testified to my family's commitment to the church. Norwegian-language church services were conducted until shortly after I was born. About the same time, the women decided to sit with their husbands instead of on opposite sides of the church, as had been the practice. My mother considered herself one of the pioneers in that respect.

I was baptized three weeks after I was born; my baptismal certificate was framed, and throughout my boyhood it hung on my bedroom wall. I was named Earl Aaron to have my father's initials. As I grew up, I got the impression that my first name was given to honor our pastor, Rev. Earl Weeks. Years later, Mother told me a different story. Before she was married she met a young mother with a cute baby boy named Earl. At that time, she says, she decided that if she ever had a boy she would give him that name. And she did. As to my middle name, Grandma Reitan insisted that I have a Biblical name. For that reason I was named Aaron, after the first high priest of Israel. My parents' aspiration that I would enter the ministry may have had some effect on the choice of my middle name.

On the day of my baptism Dad had some fun with Mother on this matter. The previous week he had played the role of Merlin in a skit presented at some social affair. Perhaps Dad was a little carried away by his thespian success. Anyway, before the baptism the practice was for the father to go to the sacristy and have a personal conference with the minister. Dad told Mother that when he met Rev. Weeks he would say that my first name would be Merlin. When Mother told me that story some years ago, her face flushed and her voice still quivered with the indignation she had felt at that moment.

"His name is Earl," she stated firmly. "I will hold the baby at the font, and when the minister asks the child's name I will give the answer." Dad lost that one, but I am inclined to believe he was only joking.

Our Grove City Home

In 1925 the modest prosperity of the Coolidge era had trickled down to places like Grove City and young families like that of Earnest and Helene Reitan. Dad had a (seemingly) steady job at the Merchants and Farmers State Bank and bought a little yellow house on a pleasant street on the south side of town. The Norwegian Lutheran church was just up the street, as was the school. For me it was a short walk with my mother down the slope and across the tracks to the bank where Daddy worked.

Photo – Earl, age four

The main entrance to the house was a covered front stoop that led into a large kitchen. In those days, people lived mainly in the kitchen, which served also as dining area and family room, to use modern terminology. One end of the kitchen had a sink, with a faucet for city water and a hand pump to draw water from the cistern. Mother cooked on a kerosene stove and baked in an oven that was placed on top of two burners. She heated water for washing and bathing in a copper boiler on top of the stove. We did not have a refrigerator until I was eleven years old; in Grove City we had an icebox with ice delivered.

The rest of the house was taken up by a small living room, and off the living room were two tiny bedrooms. There was an outside door into the living room, but it was rarely (if ever) used. There was no bathroom: people washed in a wash basin by the kitchen sink and used an outdoor privy. A hallway led to the back door.

The unfinished space upstairs was used only as an attic, which was reached by a stairway off the hallway. Dad kept his shotgun standing in the stairway; he made me a little wooden rifle to stand with it.

Mom and Dad purchased some furniture and received other items as wedding presents. Their furniture had to last them for the rest of their married life, because never again were they in a position to buy new. The living-room furniture included a large overstuffed rocking chair with arms called "The Big Chair" or "Daddy's Chair," and another rocker (not upholstered) that was "Momma's Chair." There was also a rectangular table called "The Library Table" which held a heavy table lamp. We also had a floor lamp which stood next to "The Big Chair." My parents did not have that essential item of the middle class, an upholstered sofa. Undoubtedly they intended to get one when they could afford it. The functions of a sofa were provided by an iron day bed that folded out to make an extra bed.

They had a respectable dining room set, consisting of a round dining room table with extra leaves and six dining room chairs with brown leather-covered seats. There was a matching buffet where the good china, tableware, and tablecloths were kept. The good china had little roses on it and gold edges that in due time flaked away. The silver was silverplate, of course. I have no recollection of carpets. As far back as I can recall we had linoleum on the floor, which Dad carefully varnished. There were some oval hooked rugs on the floors.

When Dad bought our house he planted a small apple tree in the back yard. It grew slowly, but eventually it produced one apple – its first. Unable to resist, I took a bamboo fishing pole and knocked the apple off. When I tasted it, it was sour. Dad was annoyed that he had lost his first apple, but he was not too upset, assuming that there would be many more in the future. The next year we moved away, so Dad never did get any apples off his tree.

I was a member of the first generation that took the automobile for granted. In the 1920s the state of Minnesota undertook an active program to build concrete highways (asphalt was uncommon then), and small towns were busy paving their streets. Although horses were still used on farms, they were no longer used for personal transportation. Dad's first car was a Model T

Ford, but in 1928 he bought a new Chevrolet for $300. He enjoyed driving it and caring for it. A good thing, too: the Depression hit the next year and he made it last until 1940.

While Dad was earning a living at the Merchants and Farmers State Bank, Mom was busy at home as a housewife and mother with three boys born within four years. Clayton was born in October 1926 and Phillip in July 1929; both were born on Sunday. We three boys grew up together as a little closed society. Although we played with other children and were in different grades in school, while we were small none of us actually had friends or activities separate from the others.

My delight in converting symbols into words began early. I had a circular dish with flat-topped sides on which were the letters of the alphabet with a picture of an animal for each letter. (L for lion, Z for zebra.) I learned all the letters and animals. I loved to sing, and one time I sang *Jesus Loves me, this I know* for a Sunday school program. Dad had a song he would sing to us boys that I now sing to my grandchildren. The words are:

Twenty froggies went to school,
Down beside a rushy pool;
Twenty little coats of green,
Twenty shirts all white and clean.

We must be on time said they.
First we work and then we play.
This must always be the rule,
When little froggies go to school.

Twenty froggies grew up fast.
They became big frogs at last.
Now they sit on other logs,
Teaching other little frogs.

The Crash

In October 1929 the New York Stock Market crashed, and in the next two years a world depression set in. The Merchants and Farmers State Bank was forced to close its doors, although eventually it paid off approximately eighty-five percent of its obligations. Dad was employed by the receiver to wind up the bank's affairs, but obviously he would have to find a new job – not an easy task with his deficient education and banks failing right and left. Fortunately, 1930 was a census year. Dad was employed by the census office in Willmar and commuted daily to his job. When the census was completed the next year he was again cast adrift.

By 1931, as the Depression deepened, all that was available was a job in Bay City, Wisconsin for $65 a month. Dad had to be satisfied with selling the house in Grove City for what he had paid for it, although he held out for a while because he thought he should make some kind of profit. Dad and Mom never owned a house again.

When they left Grove City, Mom and Dad were cut off from their roots. Grove City remained home, and they loved to go back there to visit relatives and friends. They kept their membership in the Grove City church for years thereafter. Maybe they hoped they could return some day. But the gates to the Reitan ancestral base remained permanently closed.

Bay City

When we moved to Bay City we left behind the Norwegian-American community. Our four years in Bay City seem to have been considered temporary until something better turned up. Bay City was a ragged, poverty-stricken little river town with about one hundred people. It was located on the Mississippi River where it opened into a wider body of water called Lake Pepin. Across the lake was a distinctive shoreline called Point-no-Point because it looked like a point but was not. The nearest large town was Red Wing, Minnesota, on the other side of the river. Although the Mississippi was still important for barge traffic, the boats that had stopped along its banks, as described by Mark Twain, or Jerome Kern in "Showboat", had long since disappeared.

Photo – Bay City State Bank

My recollection of the people was that they were good-natured and feckless because they had nothing to lose anyway. They were quite different from the neat and orderly Norwegian-Americans of Grove City or the sturdy, hard-working Wisconsin farmers who lived up on the plain. One source of income was fishing. The fishermen seined the river for carp that they placed in a pond kept fresh by an artesian well. There the carp were fed grain until they fattened and lost their river taste. After that they were shipped off in tank cars and sold with some fancy name, possibly Mississippi salmon. In the Depression people would eat anything that they could afford. Some jobs were provided by a mine which extracted a fine yellow sand used in glass-making. Dad eked out extra income by doing the books for the sand mine.

Since Bay City was located on the river, which was also the state line, the town was a haven for bootleggers, for Prohibition was still in effect. The booze came up the Mississippi River on boats and barges. The bootleggers hung out on a patch of dry land in the middle of the river called "the island." The bridge to Red Wing was anchored on "the island," and I recall Dad pointing out some of the bootleggers' haunts.

The Bay City business district consisted of a few ramshackle wooden buildings along an unpaved, dusty main street. At that time the gravelled main street was also the highway, which has since been moved. The railroad tracks ran parallel to the main street, a block away. The Bay City State Bank, where Dad worked, was a low brick building. The bank building has disappeared. Across the street from the bank was a one-story town hall. Between the bank and the tracks was a tiny barber shop and a crumbling old frame building that housed Hortenbach's general store.

The bank was owned by A. E. Feldman, who gave much of the responsibility for managing the bank to Dad. Small-scale Jewish businessmen were characteristic of river towns along the Mississippi and Ohio rivers, and Feldman was one of the breed. He was a hearty, genial man and we boys liked him, but Dad complained about him constantly, probably because at $65 a month he felt so exploited. Years later Mom told me that Feldman would get angry because he wanted Dad to do dishonest things, which Dad refused to do. I wonder if that included laundering the money of bootleggers.

Feldman had an attractive wife and two really pretty daughters – Beth and Bonnie – who had nice clothes and played the marimba. These girls usually stayed aloof from the overall-clad, bare-footed, riff-raff kids of Bay City, although we exhibited some traits of middle-class respectability and were occasionally invited to their house. If we had stayed in Bay City much longer I undoubtedly would have fallen in puppy love with Bonnie Feldman. Maybe I had when we left.

In addition to Dad there was a young woman named Orpha who worked in the bank doing routine bookkeeping. Both my parents liked her very much. They were pleased when she married Adolph Anderson, the husky young blacksmith, and they moved into the house next door. The night they were wed Dad told us boys to give them a charivaree (chivaree). We didn't know what that was, but Dad explained that when they had gone to bed we were to sneak under their window and make a loud noise beating pots and pans. We did so and Adolph came running angrily out of the house to see who was disturbing his wedding night. Then he spotted three little boys scurrying back to our house, and he and Dad had a good laugh about it. My Mother disapproved of exploiting little boys in this manner.

My brother Phil has a story which is an amazing example of the long memories of village people. Some years ago Phil decided to stop and see Bay City, although he was only five years old when we moved away. Nevertheless, he thought he could remember where the house was and went looking for it. As he approached it he saw a blind old man walking along the street with a white cane. He stopped the old man and asked, "Can you tell me where the Reitan (Ritten) family used to live?"

The old man, recognizing the accent and timbre of the voice exclaimed: "Ernie! Is that you, Ernie!" Forty years later he thought he heard my father's voice. When Phil explained who he was, the man patted the air with his hand about three feet above the ground and sighed: "Ah, little Phil." It is my opinion that the old man could have been none other than Adolph Anderson.

At the barber shop I made the first purchase that I can recall. Dad gave me fifty cents to buy Christmas presents for my brothers. In the barber shop I had seen a rubber pig based on Walt Disney's Three Little Pigs cartoon. When I expressed interest in buying the little pig, the barber asked me how much money I had. When I replied that I had fifty cents, he said that was exactly what it cost. (I don't know if he overcharged me or undercharged, but he was probably pleased to find a buyer for the pig.) When I got home I had a rubber pig but I had spent all my money. My folks laughed at this lack of fiscal prudence, and I made due note of my mistake.

However, all turned out well. The little rubber pig lay around the house a few years until we were older, when we discovered it could be used as a miniature football: it could be thrown in a perfect spiral and could be punted or drop-kicked with consistency. So we got a lot of fun out of it after all. Was it a good buy? Possibly when viewed from the perspective of the long-term investor.

An incident in Hortenbach's Store showed that I had learned my lesson. Mom sent me to the store to get a pound of Flame Room coffee. When I got there Hortenbach asked if I wanted the red tin, which was twenty-four cents, or the green tin, which was twenty-one cents. Having been given no instructions on that point, I took the cheaper. The hangers-on in the store laughed and told Hortenbach that I was too smart to be fooled by him. I went home with the green tin of coffee, very proud of myself. When I told Mom what had happened she accepted the coffee with thanks, but I think she probably wanted the better coffee.

Bay City was on the main line of the Burlington Railroad between Chicago and the Twin Cities, but the fast trains did not stop. I recall the excitement when the Burlington Zephyr, the first of the aluminum streamlined trains, made its maiden run. Everyone went down to the tracks to see the Zephyr flash by. It was said that the Zephyr would create such suction that children would be drawn under the wheels. As we took our places near the crossing Mom made us hold hands and stand safely back. "Whoosh" and the train was gone. I hardly saw it.

One time Dad had to go to Minneapolis on business. He got on the Zephyr for his return trip. When the conductor saw that his ticket was for Bay City, Dad was informed that the train did not stop there and he would have to go all the way to LaCrosse. Dad insisted that he had to get off in Bay City, and did so with such vehemence that the conductor stopped the train. Dad claimed he had made a mistake, but I think he just wanted to ride the Zephyr.

Dad was a feisty fellow. One time when he was driving to Minneapolis he encountered strikers who had blocked traffic into the city by putting a threshing machine belt studded with nails across the highway. Dad had learned about the strike, and he came prepared. When several of the strikers approached his car, he pulled out a pistol and told them that he had business to take care of. They pulled the belt away and let him pass. Having struggled so hard to get employment, Dad could not sympathize with anyone who had a job and refused to work.

Another time we were driving along a highway when we heard a gunshot and a pheasant fell out of the sky into the ditch. Dad immediately stopped the car, and soon a man appeared, scrambling down the bank to get his pheasant. Obviously, he was a farmer working his field who carried a shotgun on his tractor. Since it was out of season, Dad ran up to the man, pretended to be a game warden, and gave him a stern warning. Mom was quite frightened at this event, especially since the man did have a gun.

Home Life in Bay City

We lived in two different houses in Bay City. The first was an undistinguished frame box. A year or so later we moved to a pretty little bungalow overlooking the lake, probably because the bungalow was cheaper. The rent was $15 per month. It overlooked Lake Pepin, which was lower in those years than it is now. From the house a path sloped steeply down to the lake. The shoreline was not fit for swimming, and we did not have a boat, but there were lots of interesting places to play. A short distance away was a tumble-down ice house that contained cakes of ice covered by sawdust. In the summer it was a cool place to hang out.

Photo – Bay City bungalow, Lake Pepin in background

The bungalow had a front room, a kitchen, and one bedroom downstairs. There was an upstairs bedroom where Clayton and I slept in one bed. I think Phil slept in his crib in the bedroom with Mom and Dad. The upstairs window looked eastward, and I can still remember seeing wonderful pink and orange sunrises and hearing the mournful calling of the doves. There was no bathroom. We washed in a basin by the kitchen sink, and we boys took our Saturday night baths in the washtub on the kitchen floor. What my parents did about bathing, I do not know.

Our little house had an outdoor toilet, reached by walking on a pathway of planks that led from the back door. The basement was

47

a black hole that contained the furnace and coal bin, but not much else. In the basement Dad made a toilet seat with a bucket under it for us boys to use in cold weather. Years later Mom was still irritated because at times he cheated and used it himself.

The front yard had a semicircular driveway up to the house, with a pump in the center, from which we drew our water. Dad struggled in vain to maintain a lawn in front of the house, but the soil in Bay City was sandy and those were years of drought. In the front yard near the road was a large butternut tree with the shape of a hockey stick, which made it great for climbing. Today only the stump remains.

I associate that house with an important lesson. I enjoyed playing with toy cars, making roads and towns in our sandy driveway. One day a new boy turned up, whose parents travelled about repairing pots and pans. The boy, who was several years older than I, was looking for someone to play with, and he joined enthusiastically in what my brothers and I were doing. Soon he was making grandiose plans for an extended city, bossing us as we scurried to carry out his plans. "More sand," he called, "more sand," as he extended the project from the driveway into the lawn. He had left when Dad came home and found a pile of sand covering the grass in the struggling lawn he had worked so hard to achieve. We were immediately called out to rectify the damage and carry the sand away. "More sand, more sand," I now reply, when I think that my wife and family have pushed their demands too far.

Bay City was Tom Sawyer country. There were dramatic bluffs along the river and hardwood forests that were a riot of color in the fall. On warm summer evenings the side-wheeler excursion boat would come down the river from St. Paul, lights gleaming and the sounds of music and laughter drifting across the water. Up on the high ground was rolling Wisconsin farmland, with fields, pastures, and woods. Dad would take us for a ride when he had business out in the country. We loved it when he would put the car in neutral and coast down the steep hills.

In the summertime we ran barefoot, except for special occasions. For the first few days our feet were tender until they toughened, and there were always minor aggravations from stepping on a sharp stone or encountering the prickly sandburrs that infested the area. When school began it was uncomfortable to squeeze our feet back into shoes again. Most of the time, summer or winter, we wore denim bib overalls. About this time, Mom bought us jockey briefs to replace our BVDs (Minnesota translation: "button vay down.") She thought briefs were better for little boys because they kept our genitals firmly in place. In the summer getting dressed was a simple matter: I would pull on my briefs and bib overalls, grab a bite of breakfast, put my trusty cap pistol in my pocket, and go out to play.

On warm summer afternoons, Mom would take us to the fish pond, which made a great swimming hole. It was fed by an artesian well that bubbled up through an iron pipe about six inches in diameter. The water was clean and pure; it was fun to sit on top of the pipe and let the water squirt between your legs. Sometimes you could feel a carp nibble at your toes. There was one clump of willows where the girls changed their clothes and one for the boys. Sometimes the boys teased the girls by approaching their willows, only to be sent away with shrieks of rage. Nearby was a ramshackle town park with a field for softball.

Our dog Terry was an important part of life in Bay City. I don't know where Dad got him, but we were told that he was part bull terrier, a popular breed at that time. We boys loved Terry and he was devoted to us. He followed us everywhere. Dad had a special whistle which he used to call us; if we didn't hear the whistle we knew it was time to leave when Terry headed for home. One of Terry's faults was that he chased cars. Since the main road passed by the front of our yard, there were plenty for him to chase. We were never able to break him of that habit.

Across the street lived a wonderful playmate, Jimmy Reed. He was the typical freckle-faced, Norman Rockwell, all-American boy, with a big grin and a vivid imagination. Of the many things that we did with Jimmy Reed, the most memorable was when we put on a circus, with clowns, side-shows, and the like. Mom liked to sew costumes for her boys, and she made me a clown outfit. We devised a variety of acts and tricks for the main show. One of our side-shows was a swimming match, which consisted of a wooden match floating in water. There were others, but I have forgotten what they were.

Our enjoyment was dampened by Terry's misbehavior. Terry was supposed to be some kind of circus animal, but he disliked the entire idea and resisted everything we asked him to do. Finally he attacked Bonnie Feldman's little dog, whose cute paper costume he tore to shreds before starting on the dog itself. Bonnie was very upset by this, and Terry was hauled home in disgrace.

The blow fell when we went to Grove City for Dad's summer vacation and left Terry with the Reeds. When we got back the first thing we did was to run to the Reeds to get Terry. Mrs. Reed had the unhappy duty of telling us that Terry had disappeared. They had kept Terry tied up, but he had gotten loose and was never seen again. Mom stated that she would never again have a dog, because there was too much grief when something happened to it.

On Saturday afternoons we usually drove across the river to Red Wing, a beautiful small city overlooking the Mississippi and Lake Pepin. While Mom did the shopping, Dad liked to sit in the car (head-in parking at that time) and watch the people pass by. He enjoyed pointing out incongruities, such as a short man with a tall wife, or odd personal features like a misshapen hat or a grotesque handlebar mustache. He observed the passing parade with unfailing delight in human variability, but never in a cruel or nasty manner. Maybe he taught me to appreciate something about the comedie humaine that I would have missed otherwise.

Red Wing was one of the most Norwegian cities in Minnesota. It had a nice park with a swimming pool and a playground where we enjoyed the slides and swings. On one occasion we climbed the 300-odd steps to the top of Barnes' Bluff, which gave a dramatic view of the river. On the Fourth of July there were fireworks over the lake, and I recall going to see a replica of a Viking ship that had sailed across the Atlantic from Norway.

Photo – Bay City – Earl, Clayton, Phil & Terry

When we crossed the river to Red Wing we sang a song devised by University of Minnesota football fans to taunt their rivals from the University of Wisconsin, whom they dismissed as rubes from the lumber mills. In those days, the generic name for a Swede just off the boat was "Yon Yonson," a usage comparable to calling any Irishman "Paddy." The song expressed the bewilderment of a Swedish lumberjack named John Johnson when people addressed him correctly. It went:

> *Oh, my name iss Yohn Yohnson,*
> *And I come from Visconsin,*
> *I vork in da lumber mills dere.*
> *Everyvon dat I meet*
> *Says, "Hey, you wit big feet.*
> *Von't you tell uss your name?"*
>
> *And – -I – -say – – – – – .*
>
> *My name iss Yohn Yohnson*
> *And I come from Visconsin,*
> *And nobody knows my name.*
> *I nefer tell none of dem fellers,*
> *But dey call me Yohn Yohnson yust the same.*

School

A landmark in my life came in Bay City in 1931 when I started school, an institution that I loved so much that I spent the rest of my life in it.

My teacher was Miss Laura Lien, a refined young lady consigned by fate and the Depression to teaching school in Bay City. Miss Lien had a room down the street from us, but there was no decent place for her to eat. My Mother, who delighted in the presence of educated people, took her on as a boarder, and she added a great deal to our table.

I recall vividly the first day of school. The night before, Dad gave me a red pencil and carved my initials on it with his pocket-knife. The next morning, when the children were settled at their desks, Miss Lien cranked up the Victrola, played a record, and told us to march around the room. When the music stopped we were to return to our desks. I was marching proudly when the music stopped. Suddenly I realized that I did not know where my desk was. As the other children scrambled to find their places I was faced with the humiliation of being left standing alone in the aisle. Frantically I searched for my desk, but the desks all looked alike! Then I glanced down and saw the red pencil with my initials. With great relief I popped into my seat. I had passed the first test!

Photo – Bay City School

I took to reading like a duck to water. I had known my letters long before I went to school, and I can still remember how exciting it was to learn how the letters fitted together to make words. One day I was reading in my reading book when I came to the longest word I had ever seen. It stopped me for a moment, but I began sounding it out. I discovered, to my delight, that it was "e-lec-tric-i-ty."

A story that I read in my third grade reading book has lodged in my mind ever since. A sorcerer made a clay model of a man's head which, at the proper time, would speak and reveal the secret of the Philosopher's Stone. The head was put in a fiery kiln to bake. Since the Sorcerer was exhausted by his efforts, he decided to take a brief nap. He told his apprentice to be sure to awaken him the moment that the head spoke. After a while the head said: "Time is." The apprentice decided to doze a little longer. Then the head began to glow and said in an angry voice: "Time was." The apprentice became alarmed and ran to fetch the sorcerer. The head said: "Time never more shall be," and exploded.

I remember my reactions. I was indignant that the naughty apprentice had neglected his duty. I was confident that I would have run quickly to the sorcerer at the first word from the glowing head. I was sad that the secret of the Philosopher's Stone had been lost forever. Accompanying the story was an illustration, dominated by orange and blue, showing the head in the flames, the frightened apprentice rousing himself, and the sorcerer sleeping in the shadows. This image, with its foreboding words, has never left me. "Time Is – Time Was – Time never more shall be."

There were three grades in my room, and I would listen to the second and third grades when Miss Lien was teaching them. In the middle of the next year it was decided that I should skip the second grade and move to the third grade. My only problem was with arithmetic. I was told to sit with a girl named Laura who would help me. Sitting with a girl was such a disgusting experience that I did my best to get to the point where I could be on my own.

Crossing the bridge included accepting the symbols of our country, and in that respect school was very important. My schoolroom included the usual portrait of George Washington, and an American flag. We learned to stand and recite the pledge of allegiance. We observed the birthdays of George Washington ("first in war, first in peace, first in the hearts of his countrymen") and Abraham Lincoln, who, we learned, freed the slaves. At Thanksgiving we learned about Pilgrims and turkeys.

Patriotism was strengthened at home. On my bedroom wall hung a framed replica of the Declaration of Independence. How we got it I do not know, but after I learned to read I was able to make out the first few words and the big "John Hancock" on the bottom. Mom always made something with cherries on Washington's Birthday, and "the grand and glorious Fourth" was a big day, with cap pistols and firecrackers. We always observed Thanksgiving Day, too, but I do not recall having turkey. Probably we could not afford it.

Before I left the second grade I suffered a disappointing experience of the American way that remains etched in my mind. Miss Lien wanted us to learn about democracy, so she announced that there would be an election for class officers. The two candidates nominated for class president were Fritz Spriggle and myself. I was thrilled at the prospect of being elected class president, but, with typical Norwegian-American modesty, I thought it was not nice to vote for myself so I voted for Fritz.

When the ballots were counted I had lost, 13 to 12. Those numbers – 13 to 12 – have remained with me all my life. When I came home from school that day my parents could see how disappointed I was. When they asked about it, it came out that I had voted for Fritz. They laughed and assured me that there was nothing wrong with voting for myself. They pointed out that Roosevelt and Hoover had certainly voted for themselves.

The Bay City school was a county rural school and had only eight grades. There were two rooms downstairs: one for first, second, and third grades and another for fourth, fifth, and sixth grades. There was a room upstairs for the seventh and eighth grades. High school students were bused to Ellsworth, the county seat, and this situation alone convinced my Mother that Bay City was no place to raise a family. I was in fifth grade when we moved to Alberta, Minnesota, and it was quite a shock to me to find out how far behind I was.

Church

The Lutheran Church was always an important part of our lives. For Sunday worship we drove up the slope, past the sand mine, into the countryside to a plain little Swedish Lutheran church called Tabor. The members were mainly Scandinavian farmers – our kind of people. My parents did not become members, because it was not our synod and also (I think) because our residence in Bay City was considered to be temporary.

Sunday school, of course, was part of churchgoing. I remember a time when we had a Sunday school lesson about the creation of Eve from the rib of Adam. Someplace I had gotten the idea that women have one more rib than men, and I asked the teacher if that was the reason why. She laughed so hysterically that she almost had to dismiss the class.

An incident that I still recall with some embarrassment sheds light on my determination not to be found doing something wrong. One Sunday, when the collection plate was passed, I could not find the two pennies that were my standard contribution to the Sunday school. I felt terribly embarrassed and ashamed, thinking that surely someone had noticed. I was convinced it was sinful to go to Sunday school and not pay. I did not dare tell my parents of the awful thing that had happened.

The next Sunday Dad gave me the usual two pennies. When I reached in the side pocket of my jacket for my contribution, I also found the pennies of the Sunday before. I did not want to put four pennies on the plate, for fear someone would notice and ask about it, in which case I would have to confess my sin of the previous Sunday. Of course I would never think of doing anything as sinful as spending the Lord's money for candy. After Sunday school, when no one was looking, I surreptitiously threw the extra two pennies under a bush. What that tells about me I can't say for certain, but I don't think it is good.

At Christmas time the church was decorated with a big Christmas tree and the Sunday school children put on a Christmas program. Each child was required to memorize a poem or Bible verse and recite it for the assembled congregation. The most enjoyment was derived from the tiny tots, who were given a push toward the front by the teacher, turned shyly toward the audience, and usually recited their "piece" so rapidly and in such a low voice that they could not be heard. Then they ran back to their place in the front pew. Being something of a showoff, I always enjoyed doing my recitation and spoke up in a bright, clear voice.

A common feature of these Sunday school Christmas programs was a pageant, culminating in a manger scene with Mary (always a blond girl) and Joseph (always a tall boy). Smaller girls served as angels wearing wings of silvery paper; boys were shepherds wearing hooded-gowns made of gunny sacks or Wise Men wearing colorful bathrobes. The manger scene was usually accompanied by singing of the appropriate carol as the characters appeared. *It Came Upon a Midnight Clear* was appropriate for the shepherds. One time I was a Wise Man and sang, with two other boys, *We Three Kings of Orient Are*.

Another Christmas program brought one of those petty challenges which can be so important to a small boy. I was one of three shepherds in the pageant. In our scene I was supposed to light a small candle which, covered by a piece of red glass, was concealed in some firewood. The candle would help us look like shepherds huddled around a fire on a cold night in the desert.

I had never struck a match before; I had been strictly forbidden to touch or play with matches in any way. I knew how to strike a match, but I was filled with nervous tension as I prepared to light the candle. My first try did not succeed, but on the second try the match flared and I lit the candle. I felt both proud and relieved.

Bible stories at bedtime were an important part of my childhood. Since I was small and easily pushed around by bigger, rougher boys, I liked David and Goliath. Another of my favorites was Ehud, one of the more obscure judges, who stabbed the Midianite king. Ehud gained admittance to the king's tent because he was left-handed and the guards neglected to check the right side of his body for his dagger. I liked to think that my left-handedness might someday be an advantage, but I don't think it ever was.

Boyhood Interests

Learning to read opened up a thrilling new world, and I soon became an omnivorous reader. One of my favorites was a book entitled Old Greek Stories. I still remember the illustration of Greek warriors springing up from dragon's teeth. A continuing feature of my boyhood days was the Saturday afternoon trip to the library to check out books. Bay City had no library, but Mom regularly took us to the public library in Red Wing. I was very annoyed when I asked for a splendid copy of "Don Quixote" that was locked in a glass case. The librarian solicitously told me that the book was not for little boys, and the memory of that rejection still rankles.

Mom, always aware of modern ideas of child raising, got me a subscription to *Boy's Life*, the magazine of the Boy Scouts of America. I loved that magazine, which contained short stories about boys, articles about the Boy Scout movement, and cartoons. Perhaps because I was small, I especially liked a series of stories about the Mudhen, a clever lad who outfoxed the bigger boys. Unfortunately, I had no opportunities to be a Boy Scout. There were no Boy Scouts in any of the tiny towns that we lived in, and we probably couldn't have afforded a uniform and all that attractive equipment anyway.

One of the ways that Dad maintained continuity with Minnesota was by continuing his subscription to the Minneapolis *Journal*, which came by mail, one day late. My life-long love affair with newspapers began with Dad reading the comics to us boys. When I learned to read I would spread the paper out on the floor and read the comics to Clayton and Phil, until they learned to read for themselves.

Soon I was reading the sports pages. The sports editor was Dick Cullom, whose daily stint was predictably called "Cullom's Column." I recall telling my parents that Max Baer would beat Carnera for the heavyweight championship (1934). They asked me how I knew, and laughed when I said "Dick Cullom told me." I recall reading about the retirement of Babe Ruth. The big story, of course, was the Minnesota Gophers under their great football coach, Bernie Bierman.

Another important learning experience came at age nine, when I began violin lessons. The Reitans and Jensens were musical, and it was expected that I would sing or play an instrument. As long as I can remember I had been indoctrinated with the idea that the greatest of all instruments was the violin. Aunt Rose was especially insistent on this point, and gave me a violin that had been in the family.

Ole Bull, the Norwegian violinist, was regarded with great reverence. One time Dad received a certificate for a free night at the King Cole hotel in Minneapolis. He took us boys with him. Across the street was a park which had a statue of Ole Bull. When

Dad pointed out the statue he declared that Ole Bull was the greatest violinist who ever lived – the Norwegian point of view, of course! Thus it was foreordained that I would play the violin, and I saw no reason (then or now) to question the high esteem in which this splendid instrument is held.

My teacher's name was Irving Venberg. He charged fifty cents and came to our house every Saturday morning to give the lesson. He was a quiet, dark-faced, thin-haired man with long delicate fingers. He lived with his parents in the country. It is my belief that he was a professional musician left unemployed by the Depression.

On the Sunday afternoon after my first lesson, Mom sat at the dining room table counting as I played whole notes and half notes on the A and D strings. Venberg put little strips of paper on the neck of the violin to help me with fingering. By the time the pieces of paper had worn away, my fingers knew where to go.

My violin book was called "A Tune a Day", and included many duets, which Venberg would play with me. I still remember his strong, warm tone. In that year of violin lessons I got to the last page of Book I, which consisted of simplified themes from classical works, including the theme from the first movement of the Beethoven violin concerto. Much later, Mom recalled that I had worked extra hard on those themes. I suspect that my violin playing was about to take off, but then we moved away.

Firearms early came into my life. Dad was an enthusiastic hunter and a crack shot. The hunting around Bay City was not good for pheasants, although there were lots of ducks. I wanted an air rifle very much and put on a campaign to get one for Christmas. I recall coming down on Christmas morning to check my stocking, fully expecting to get my wish. The stockings were hung in a rather dark corner. My stocking contained the usual oranges, hard candy, etc., but nothing special. My brothers had good presents but I had none.

Then Dad asked me how I liked my present from Santa Claus. I said I hadn't gotten very much, so he told me to look in the corner. There, somewhat out of sight, was a Daisy air-rifle, Buck Jones model. I was thrilled. Dad took me down in our basement and set up a target. I fired several times but hit nothing. When I complained that my gun didn't shoot straight, Dad fired it and put two pellets right in the bullseye. So it seemed that the rifle was OK. After that I went outside and tried my air rifle on sparrows, who did not seem to be much affected, even when I hit them, which was rarely.

It was in Red Wing that I attended the first movie of which I have any specific recollection: John Bowles and Ruby Keeler in "Forty-Second Street". I liked cowboy movies, because they had plenty of adventure, hard riding, fighting, and shooting, without romance. I was at that age when little boys don't like "love stuff." Whenever kissing took place or seemed imminent, I covered my eyes.

On one such occasion, I heard the audience laugh.

"What happened?," I asked my mother.

"Didn't you see?," she replied, "the girl slapped him."

"No," I admitted, "I covered my eyes."

On the way home, I took a ribbing about that, and was advised to keep my eyes open so I didn't miss something.

I also recall the purchase of our first radio. It was a Brunswick with the shape of a half-oval. It cost thirteen dollars. The model without a light behind the dial was a dollar cheaper. I listened intently while Mom and Dad debated whether they should buy the cheaper model. I was glad when they decided to get the radio with the lighted dial.

The radio was an important influence in the assimilation of a Norwegian-American family, and it added an important new dimension to my life. It sat in the front room on the library table. In the late afternoon I listened to children's programs such as "Jack Armstrong", "Buck Rogers", "Skippy Skinner", and "Little Orphan Annie". From the radio I learned to sing snatches of the popular songs of the day, among them *Yes, We Have no Bananas*, Kate Smith's theme song, *When the Moon Comes over the Mountain*, and a sweet, nostalgic melody, *There's an Old Spinning Wheel in the Parlor*.

"Buck Rogers" also appeared in the comic strips. One consequence was that I became quite comfortable with the solar system, for Buck and his companions in their rocket ship flitted among the planets, each of which had a civilization of its own, adapted to its size and climate. Sometimes they proceeded under the power of their rocket engine, and some times on their "momentum." I did not know what momentum was, so I assumed that the momentum was a lesser kind of engine. Anyway, "Buck Rogers" made me a citizen of the universe.

It is safe to say that children of my age were the first members of the media generation. We were also media victims. One time my Mother showed Mrs. Reed some silver-plate tablespoons that she had gotten with coupons from Wheaties. Mrs. Reed was shocked that we could afford to buy Wheaties. My Mother admitted that we really couldn't afford them, adding that the boys listened to "Jack Armstrong" and insisted on having Wheaties to grow up strong. I remembered that incident years later, when I heard Uncle Maurice say that he would never eat Wheaties because "they take advantage of a bunch of dumb kids."

One of the programs we liked best was "Gangbusters", which began with sirens, squealing tires, tommy guns, and other sounds associated with crime. Each program told the story of some criminal and how he was captured. At the end came "The Clues," which informed listeners of the most-wanted criminals and gave clues to use in helping the police capture them. From "Gangbusters" we learned about J. Edgar Hoover and the G-Men, John Dillinger, "Baby-face" Nelson, "Pretty Boy Floyd," "Soup" Grayson (who carried a container of nitroglycerine with him on his crimes), and other notorious criminals. Their adventures gave us ideas that we used when we played our favorite game: "cops and robbers."

This was the age of bank robbers like Bonnie and Clyde that I knew about from "Gangbusters". The little Bay City bank, located in an isolated area and in a town with no law enforcement officials, was an obvious target. One afternoon I was walking home from school when a lady called out to me that the bank had been robbed. I had to pass the bank to get to our house, and as I approached I saw a group of men in front of the bank whom I assumed were the robbers. I turned down an alley to avoid them and ran home. When I arrived, breathlessly, no one was there. I thought everyone had been kidnapped. I was standing in the living room crying when Mom, who had rushed to the bank with Clayton and Phil, realized that I would be coming back from school and hurried home to get me.

The story was that two gunmen entered the bank shortly before closing. They took the money, locked (they thought) Feldman, Orpha, and Dad into the vault, and then left in a getaway car parked outside. What the robbers did not know was that the vault had a protective catch so that it would not lock unless the catch was purposely released. In the vault was a big horse-pistol. As the robbers rushed out, Dad opened the vault door and fired one shot inside the bank that left a bullet-hole in the wall. Then he ran into the street and emptied the pistol in their general direction as they sped away in a cloud of dust.

Dad winged one of the robbers, who went to a doctor in Red Wing the next day, claiming a farm accident. The doctor recognized a gunshot wound and, knowing of the Bay City robbery, called the police. Dad identified the man as one of the robbers and he was convicted. The leader of the gang was apprehended in Seattle a year or more later and brought back to Minneapolis for trial. He had a long list of charges, and Dad also testified at his trial.

Photo – Red Wing Mn. Mississippi River Bridge from Minnesota shore, Wisconsin in background *c.* 1920.

Every year Dad received one week's vacation, which we used for a visit to Grove City. Early in the morning we would set off in our 1928 Chevy, the three boys in the back. At Hastings, Minnesota we traversed an amazing wooden bridge shaped like a corkscrew. In Grove City we stayed at Grandma Jensen's house, which was on the same street as our former house. Uncle Gust and Aunt Florence and their brood lived a short distance down the alley in back. Of course we stopped at Atwater to see Aunt Rose and Uncle Ben, and we also visited Aunt Beattie and Uncle Maurice. The other Reitans had left Grove City long ago. The visit always included a stop at the Jensen family farm, where Uncle Christ, Aunt Vera, and their three boys lived. Martin, Art, Carl and Emmanuel also lived in the area, and they all might gather on a Sunday afternoon at Grandma Jensen's house.

Photo – Hastings, Mn. Spiral Bridge *c.* 1915

Although Mom had adapted to Bay City reasonably well, Dad still thought of Grove City as home. The trip invariably included visits downtown, three little boys in tow, where Dad was greeted as someone who still belonged there but had, for some reason, been away for a while. The building that had housed the former Merchants and Farmers State Bank had been converted into the Larson sisters' ice cream store, and we would stop there for cones. Upstairs was Aunt Hilda, who was "Central" until her health failed. On Sunday morning we got dressed up and went to church, just as if we had never been away. We always took a walk up to the graveyard, a cheerful place on a summer's day, with the breeze murmuring through the pines.

Leaving Childhood

In February 1935, Dad announced that we were moving. He had a new job as cashier of a small bank in Alberta, Minnesota, about eighty miles north and west of Grove City. The job was a step up for Dad, who would be running his own bank and no longer in servitude to Feldman. Mom was pleased because Alberta had a good school and a Norwegian Lutheran church. Both were glad to be going back to Minnesota and their own kind.

Before we left, the people of Bay City, always ready to enjoy themselves, held a going-away party for us in the town hall. It was a dance, although my parents did not dance and Mother thought dancing led to wickedness, which at times it did. They gave us an end table which my parents used for the rest of their married life. To my knowledge, we never kept in touch with any of our Bay City friends. From the beginning, we had been outsiders and transients.

Photo – Lake Pepin in foreground, Point-no-Point in background on right, from the Bay City community park.

Bay City was a paradise for boys. I was six when we moved there and ten when we left. In Bay City I lived a Mark Twain existence – a red-haired, freckle-faced, barefoot boy in overalls, accompanied everywhere by two younger brothers and a faithful dog. The school was undemanding, but once I learned to read I began educating myself about things that interested me. In back of our house was the mighty Mississippi, relaxing in the embrace of Lake Pepin, and still unvanquished by the lock-and-dam projects that eventually turned it into a series of sluggish pools. The mysterious outlines of Point-no-Point loomed in the distance. In the other direction were hills, woods, and noble bluffs pockmarked with caves. Bay City gave me four of the happiest years of my life.

One day in February 1935, a cattle truck with three husky young men arrived at our house. The Grove City furniture, augmented by our new end table, was loaded into the truck and we set off in our 1928 Chevrolet, followed by the truck, which arrived at our house in Alberta shortly after we did. Our Alberta house was larger than our Bay City bungalow, and our meager furniture fitted in rather nicely. It was cold outside and my brothers and I stayed in the house, although several boys (eager for new playmates) wanted us to come outside.

We boys did not want to move, and we hoped that some day we would return to our Bay City home. Several months after we had moved, Dad reported with an air of triumph that Feldman wanted him back and had made a fair offer. We were thrilled at the possibility, but Mom scotched that idea quickly, saying in no uncertain terms: "We're not going back to Bay City with our heads hanging like whipped dogs!"

Our stay in Bay City had no discernible influence on my parents, who remained the same small-town, Norwegian-Americans that they were before. For me, the move to Alberta marked the end of my unthinking, carefree childhood. In "Fern Hill" Dylan Thomas wrote of a similar happy boyhood, dashed by the realities of growing up:

> Now as I was young and easy under the apple boughs
> About the lilting house and happy as the grass was green .
> . .
> Time let me hail and climb
> Golden in the heydays of his eyes . . .
> Time held me green and dying
> Though I sang in my chains like the sea.

THE SECOND GENERATION:
A STEP AHEAD, A STEP BACK
(1935-1942)

Alberta

Alberta was a typical Minnesota tank town along a branch railroad and a secondary highway. The town was unusually deprived in that it was a tank town without a water tank. Without city water, we had to use the town pump, which was just a block from our house. Alberta seems to have been a case of arrested development. Apparently plans to install city water had foundered some time earlier. Curbs and sidewalks had been installed in places, but the work had not been completed by paving the streets. When we arrived in 1935, Alberta was an unfinished small town lying stagnant in the Depression.

Like most small towns of its type, Alberta was built along the railroad tracks, with the usual depot, gasoline storage tanks, and several grain elevators. It was always a thrill to see a powerful steam engine at work. The call of the steam whistle approaching a road crossing (especially in the middle of a winter night) had a plaintiveness that only those who have heard it can appreciate. In addition to the freight train, a little train for passengers and mail ("the dinky") came through at 5:30 P.M. – the signal to quit playing and go home for supper.

The business street was one-block long, with the bank, a squat brick building, on one corner. Next door was a small frame cream station to collect cream and eggs from farmers (Alberta did not have a creamery). The business street also included two stores, Bill Braun's gas station/garage, Bob Treischel's cafe, a barber shop, and Joe Ludwig's beer parlor in a converted railroad club car. In the middle of the block was a ramshackle two-story frame building that housed a pool hall, with apartments upstairs. It was covered with black tarpaper, so we called it "the black building" in mocking allusion to the Black Building, one of the main buildings of Fargo and the site of radio station WDAY.

Photo – Alberta State Bank, converted into a tavern.

Jack Schultz's Store, across from the bank, was a general store, based mainly on groceries but including dabs of clothing, shoes, and what were called "notions." Schultz was in his mid-fifties when we arrived in Alberta; he was rotund, gregarious, and slow-moving. His wife was lean and active. She and their eldest son, Lee, probably did most of the work in the store.

In those days before self-service, most of the food items were behind the counter, and the storekeeper fetched whatever the customer asked for. One time I bought six peppermint cigarettes for a penny, and asked Lee if he would put them in a bag. He complied, remarking ruefully: "There goes my profit."

L. M. Larson's Store, at the other end of the block, was a grocery only, but it also had the post office. Since Schultz and Larson were both stockholders in the bank, we tried to divide our purchases equally, but Schultz's store was closer to our house and inevitably got more of our trade. Larson was tall and distinguished in appearance, with the easy sociability of the shopkeeper. He was a member of our church, where he was the largest contributor. (I know, because Dad counted the collection.) The gala wedding of his attractive younger daughter, Verna, was the grandest social event of the Depression-plagued years that we lived there.

Mother viewed Joe Ludwig's Saloon with great disapproval, although Dad was always sympathetic to Joe, who was a pleasant enough fellow and a customer of the bank. I felt great anxiety on the several times that I went in there to distribute posters. The air was thick with stale tobacco smoke and the sickly-sweet smell of beer. Joe himself was a cadaverous person, with a sallow complexion, sunken chest, and watery eyes. He had sold his health to Demon Rum but he made a living, no small feat in the Depression.

By the town pump was a blacksmith shop operated by a fierce-looking, heavy-set, mustachioed old man named Bangarter. He wore a grimy leather cap and apron, and looked as if he rarely washed. He shoed horses, repaired wagons, etc. To my knowledge, he never left his house and the adjoining shop. I felt considerable anxiety when Dad sent me there to have a chisel sharpened. I was intrigued by the glowing forge and the clutter of old tools and metal parts, but I was relieved when he silently handed back the chisel and I could hurry home. Every day at noon his sweet little old wife went to Joe Ludwig's with a covered tin pail to get beer for dinner. It was said that sometimes at night screams were heard coming from the house when he beat her.

The population of Alberta was about 125. In this part of Minnesota the Norwegian-American influence had thinned out considerably. The people were a mix of Germans and Scandinavians, with a few ordinary Americans thrown in. Alberta was located in that transitional area where Minnesota merges into the plains of South Dakota, then suffering the worst consequences of the Depression and the Dust Bowl. The town was barren and dusty; the trees were small and the grass thin and patchy. There was a town hall and a town park, but otherwise amenities were lacking.

The nearest town of any size was Morris, the county seat. Morris had a business street of several blocks that included two banks, a J. C. Penney store, Woolworth's, and a spanking new movie theater. There was a public library where we went during our Saturday afternoon shopping trips to check out books. The town also had a weekly newspaper, an agricultural extension campus of the University of Minnesota, the Stevens County fairground, and a park with an artificial lake where we could go swimming in the summer. Towns like Litchfield, Red Wing, and Morris, with populations of one to two thousand, shaped my idea of a city; I thought it would be wonderful to live in such a place.

The Alberta State Bank

For Dad, Alberta was a good move. He was pleased to be in charge of a bank and free from the tyranny of Feldman. The bank was small and the salary was low, but this was the career that Dad had expected to pursue. He genuinely enjoyed his job and worked hard at it. The bank had a checkered history and was virtually defunct when Dad took it over in 1935, but by 1942 it was making some money.

With Dad's new and improved status, Mom achieved an objective that she had sought for years. Dad had always worn a cloth cap, but she persuaded him that he should wear a hat. So he got a felt fedora suitable for a banker, which added both to his dignity and his height. However, he went hatless when weather permitted.

Dad understood well the routine operations of small rural banks, and he could manage the loans and services that such banks provided for local businessmen and farmers. He often clerked for auctions, of which there were many in those Depression days. The bank had four stockholders, among them the two storekeepers, Schultz and Larson. Dad was assisted in the bank by Julene Schultz, daughter of Jack. When I was in sixth grade, Dad gave me a job sweeping the bank after school and increasased my allowance from ten cents to twenty-five cents per week.

The bank was redolent of varnished wood, sweeping compound, oil for the accounting machines, tobacco smoke, and humanity in general. Dad or Julene dealt with customers behind a stand-up counter with a brass lattice-work teller's window, and a four-inch fringe of frosted glass running along the top. In one corner Dad kept an oleander tree. There were several spittoons, and they were used for that purpose. The money and books were kept in a metal-lined vault with a thick, imposing door and combination locks. Dad had his own desk and typewriter in the back room.

It was an important day when the state bank examiners came to town. Dad was proud that the bank was always in apple-pie order and that the examiners were able to breeze through the job in a couple of hours. Of course, there was so little business that there wasn't much for them to examine.

Life could be tough for bankers during the Depression. People didn't pay their debts, and they got angry when Dad had to demand payment. However, Dad was good natured, and he realized that he could not get blood out of a stone. I am not aware that he ever foreclosed a mortgage. Dad sometimes talked about these things at the dinner table, and this family table-talk helped indoctrinate into me the importance of managing money carefully.

His main headache was L. M. Larson's hard-bitten elder daughter, Lucille, who operated, with her husband, a struggling store\gas station at Herman, about twenty-five miles north of Alberta. Since her father was a principal stockholder of the Alberta State Bank, Lucille expected privileges not given to others and wrote checks with insufficient funds that Dad, with his strict financial probity, regularly bounced. Since Larson was a principal stockholder, Lucille turned these business matters into nasty rows.

Late one afternoon, when Dad was putting up the awning at closing time, someone came up behind him, he said, and hit him on the head. Dad was momentarily stunned and fell to the sidewalk. He was convinced that Lucille's husband had hit him with a blackjack, and he filed charges with the sheriff. Since there were no witnesses, the man was released. Phil recalls seeing him return to town, waving his arms in a gesture of triumph.

Nothing happened to the Alberta bank as exciting as the daylight holdup in Bay City, although burglars did burrow into the vault at night. They broke open safe-deposit boxes and scattered papers on the floor, but they were frustrated by the safe. The state police attributed the break-in to a gang of burglars that had been operating in that part of the state, but Dad thought it was somebody local, and he thought he knew who it was. The fact that they could not crack the safe suggested local amateurs.

Another time a young man named Clark Roberts, who was having money problems and had gotten raging drunk, charged into the bank and challenged Dad to a fight. Dad told Roberts to come out into the street. Clayton, who was taking afternoon coffee to the bank, as we often did in the summer, saw Dad backing out of the door, fists up Jim Corbett style, with Roberts after him. Roberts took a swing and gave Dad a shove, and Dad fell backward, hitting his head on the sidewalk. Dad got shaken up pretty badly, and I don't think he did any damage to Roberts, but then Roberts was twenty years younger.

As for Mom, Alberta meant a little more money, a bigger house, a Norwegian Lutheran Church, and most important of all, a good school. After some heart-searching, my parents transferred their membership from Grove City to the Alberta congregation. Dad always counted and deposited the collection after church, and Mom sang in the choir and was active in the Ladies Aid society. Dad became town clerk and was on the school board. He also served as an adviser to the local 4-H club. In their minds, Bay City had always been a temporary way-station, and they settled down to spend the rest of their lives in Alberta which, after all, was the kind of Minnesota small town that they knew.

Our House

We rented a house a block from the bank for twenty dollars per month. The house was owned by the Alberta Building and Loan Association, which was defunct except for the house, its only asset. We called this shadowy firm "The Leave the Building Alone," because it had no money with which to fix anything. Dad did occasional repairs around the house, but as renters we had no reason to do any major improvements.

Photo – Alberta, Mn – Our house. Taken in 1980s

Finally we had adequate room for our furniture. In the front were a living room and a dining room, each covered with a nine-by-twelve linoleum rug. In back were the kitchen, a bedroom where Mom and Dad slept, and the bathroom. Behind the kitchen was a room where the washing machine was set up. The furnace was in the basement; the heated air rose naturally through one main register and several smaller registers in the floor and diffused itself throughout the house. In the back yard was garden space and a tumble-down garage. There were three bedrooms upstairs, but at first we boys slept in the large bedroom. Later I got my own room.

Mother was responsive to the latest ideas about home-making, one of which was that children should have their own beds instead of sleeping two in a bed, which was common in those days. As soon as we arrived in Alberta she ordered three metal beds from Montgomery Ward, with sheets and mattresses, which she placed in the large bedroom. This step was considered very "advanced," since we were all males and could just as well share beds.

Our house faced the main street, which had a sidewalk and curb but was not paved. Across the street was a vacant lot, and behind that lot was a junk yard where Bill Braun kept old farm machinery. We boys would play a form of baseball by batting stones across the street into the vacant lot. Any stone hit into Bill Braun's derelict farm machinery was a home run. We also played on the vacant lot. It was there that we discovered that the little pig made a perfect football.

Between the street and the sidewalk was a terrace that was planted with struggling boxelder trees. In the summer these trees became infested with boxelder bugs, which were an ugly nuisance. As usual, Dad tried to keep a front lawn, but three boys using it for play (plus the drought) made that difficult. Our trash and ashes were dumped in the alley in the back. Every several weeks Dad would borrow a trailer and we would haul it out to the town dump.

The winters of 1935 and 1936 were unusually severe, and our little town on the prairie was whipped by fierce blizzards. Stinging snow polluted by powdery dust from plowed fields blotted out the sun and crept into the house through cracks around the windows and doors. Our basement was a black hole that contained a coal bin and a coal-burning furnace; the heated air rose naturally through a central register and from there diffused itself unevenly throughout the house. On the worst nights our upstairs bedrooms could become dangerously cold, and on such occasions we would sleep in the living room.

Norma

In September 1936 a baby sister joined our family; like her brothers, she arrived on Sunday. Norma was the only one of the children to be born in a hospital. A day or two later, Dad drove us boys to Morris to see Mother and our new sister. We were not much impressed by our sister, but Mom was luxuriating in the cleanliness, order, and comfort of her cheery hospital room. In those days mothers stayed in the hospital for seven days. That was probably the longest period of rest Mother ever enjoyed until she retired. Dad assured her that things were well in hand at home.

In some ways they were. Dad had his own way of making tasty, juicy hamburgers, which were put on Mom's homemade white bread with a slice of onion. I recall one night when he made hamburgers, and another night when Bob Treischel, who operated the cafe, gave us two quarts of maple nut ice cream. We had never had so much ice cream at one time and we stuffed ourselves on that. Ladies from the church brought us hot dishes. One way or another, we were well fed.

The morning that Mom was to come home, we got busy and cleaned the house, although I admit we did a rather hurried job. Since we did not have time to wash the accumulated dishes before school, we piled them on the kitchen table. A week's laundry, of course, had not been done. When Mom got home she was shocked to find how much housework awaited her. Dad prudently hurried off to the bank, and we boys went back to school. Mom was very crabby for several days thereafter.

Although Mom and Dad were happy that they finally had a girl, the prospect of another child to maintain must have caused some concern. Additionally Dad was faced with the recent cost of moving plus the expenses of childbirth. One day Dad asked me to sit down with him in the back room of the bank. He told me that when I was born he had taken out a $1,000 life insurance policy for me with Mutual of New York. He needed the money, he said, and had cashed in the policy. He would get me another policy, he added, when times were better.

Of course, that never happened, but I bear no grudge. He needed the money more than I needed $1,000 of life insurance. I have lived a long time, and I would hate to think of having paid premiums all those years with nothing to show for them. Paying for Norma was a much better use of our scant resources.

As the eldest, I was called on to help out in the house and with the baby. I never changed Norma's diapers, which would violate the modesty which was part of our lives, but I did almost everything else that a baby requires. I have a vivid recollection of hanging out diapers on a windy afternoon. When I got my own children, I found that I had good skills in parenting, and that early exposure may have helped.

Family Life

In our family life and routines we considered ourselves middle class. Because we believed that we were "respectable," we managed to live like respectable people on an income that would be well below the poverty level today. Our narrow lifestyle was an essential survival technique for people who lived one step away from disaster, defined as being unemployed and having to go on "relief." As the banker, Dad knew as well as anyone (and perhaps better than the minister) the earthly wages of sin. Our family had to be rigorously functional: we could not afford waste, self-indulgence, ill health, bad debts, or trouble of any kind. Somehow, we boys knew that, although no one had actually told us.

Dad's salary was low but it came every month, which in the Depression set us apart from many people. We were always able to pay our bills, but then we spent modestly and NEVER bought on time payments. As was customary in small towns in those days, we charged our groceries at Schultz's and Larson's stores and Dad paid the bill at the end of the month, receiving a bag of candy for the kiddies as a bonus. We relied heavily on the Montgomery Ward catalog for clothing and other family needs. The catalog, with its wide array of goods, was an education in itself, and the arrival of a new catalog was an event.

As respectable people, we always presented a decent appearance. Five days a week we boys went off to school with hands-face-neck-ears (Mom's checklist) washed, hair combed, teeth brushed, toileted, and ready for the day. Three times daily we sat down to a cooked meal at the usual times and said grace before we ate. Our house was clean and neat, and Dad did his best to maintain the yard. We did not swear or use bad language of any kind, nor did we tell off-color jokes. We did not have loud family shouting-matches; whatever differences Mom and Dad had, they settled quietly between themselves. We were not shrinking violets, but our family ethos was clear: never show off, never toot your own horn, and never accept food the first time it is offered.

Our clothes were washed and ironed once a week. We took a bath every Saturday night "whether we needed it or not," as the saying went. We then put on clean pajamas, which in those parts was another of Mother's middle-class affectations, since many men and boys slept in their underwear. On Sunday morning we got a clean shirt and clean underwear and socks to wear to church and for several days after that. In those days before Kleenex, when we had a cold we used a handkerchief, which soon became sopping wet. Many men and boys wiped their noses on their sleeves or, if outdoors, just let fly, which led Dad to pose the riddle: "What is it that the rich man keeps and the poor man throws away?"

We never had a telephone. We thought of a telephone call as an emergency. If people needed to call us, they called the bank. There was no idea that Mother might wish to chat with friends on a telephone, and even less that the boys might use a phone. Mother did not drive the car either, and insisted that she did not want to drive. Without a telephone or car, her life was confined to the house, the family, and to people or places that she could reach on foot.

The usual fare at breakfast was oatmeal with toast, although sometimes we had cold cereal or eggs. Dinner, with meat, potatoes, gravy, and dessert was at noon. Dad closed the bank from 12:00 to 1:00 for this purpose, and we boys walked home from school. Supper was a lighter meal, often consisting of leftovers or cheap but filling food like soup or pancakes. Bedtime was about 9:00 p.m.

Mom's challenge was to feed her family at minimal cost. A typical dinner was a pound of hamburger in the form of meat loaf with potatoes and vegetables. Mom also made a good baked spaghetti with a pound of hamburger and her own home-canned tomato sauce. Another common meal was a pound of round steak pounded with flour to make it tender and then cooked in gravy. A meaty soup bone with plenty of vegetables and home-baked bread would make a meal. In the Depression, canned salmon was cheap. A can would make a meal when served as salmon loaf, salmon patties, or salmon croquettes. Baked chicken was a common Sunday dinner. Other Depression-era tummy-stuffers were baked beans, Velveeta sandwiches fried in a skillet, and ring bologna with boiled potatoes. Mom rarely made typical Scandinavian food, except at Christmas, when she made flat bread, rosettes, and special cookies. We had lutefisk on Christmas Eve.

We had plenty of potatoes, carrots, beets, peas, beans and tomatoes from our garden, which Mom canned along with crates of peaches and plums when they appeared in the store. When winter came the shelves in the basement were lined with filled mason jars. Mom's specialty was baking, and we had plenty of homemade bread, cinnamon rolls, cakes, and cookies. The only exception to our modest fare came during hunting season, when we had an abundant supply of pheasant and duck. On occasion we boys pleaded for hamburgers or bologna for a change from pheasant.

Needless to say, we never ate out, except for an occasional hot dog and root beer. Among the things we never had in the house were catsup, soda pop, or ice cream. Of course, beer and hard liquor never crossed our doorstep, except on New Years' Day, when Dad would smuggle in some drinkable alcohol that could be detected in his flushed face and lively manner.

Lacking an older daughter, Mom assigned us boys housework. We began with washing dishes, taking turns doing the washing, which was more work than drying. Every Saturday morning I had several chores. One was to mix a cake or a batch of cookies. Mom did the actual baking. Clayton made bread, or at least mixed the dough. It was also my responsibility to scrub the kitchen floor. All three of us boys ended up handy with cooking and housework, thanks to this early training.

It is difficult to maintain respectability without an adequate water supply, but we managed. The water pail stood in the pantry, and one of my tasks was to keep it filled. Every morning, even in the coldest winter weather, I went to the town pump and lugged home a bucket of fresh water. On washday we borrowed milk cans from the little cream station next to the bank. We filled these cans at the town pump, put them in our coaster wagon, and pulled them home for wash water.

Washing three loads of laundry was a big job. Mom heated the water in a copper boiler on the kerosene stove. She used brown Fels-Naptha soap, which she shaved into chips with a paring knife. The washing machine had a hand-operated wringer. When possible, clothes were hung with wooden clothespins on a clothesline in the back yard, which gave them a wonderful freshness when they were blown by the wind. In the winter they would freeze stiff, but they would eventually dry. On a rainy Monday, Mom would have to wash and dry them in small batches, drying them on a folding rack inside the house.

Another source of water was the cistern, a large cavity dug into the ground and lined with concrete. It was fun to shout into the cistern and hear the reverberations. Cisterns were dangerous, and occasionally one would hear of a child that had fallen into a cistern and drowned. The cistern collected rainwater, although in those years of drought rainwater was scarce. The kitchen sink had a hand pump to draw cistern water, which was heated on the stove for washing dishes. The bank also had a cistern, and we brought soft water home from there, again using the milk cans and coaster wagon. Water for cooking was brought from the town pump.

Unlike many houses in Alberta, our house had an indoor bathroom with basin, bathtub, and flush toilet, but since there was no city water the usefulness of these facilities was greatly diminished. On Saturday night, Mom would heat the bath water on the stove, and we would carry it to the bathtub. We were better off than many, in that we had a stool in the bathroom. However, the cistern water was too scarce to use for flushing. A bucket was kept in the bathroom, and Saturday night bath water was used for that purpose. Next we used Monday's wash water. The system was crude, but it was better than carrying flush water from the town pump or going outside to a privy, as many people in Alberta did.

School

When we moved to Alberta, the luck of the draw brought us to a school that was a pet project of the state Department of Education. The Minnesota legislature, seeking ways to move rural education beyond the one-room schoolhouse, had offered grants to encourage consolidation of rural school districts into larger units that could support a high school and maintain better facilities. In 1911 the Alberta school and a neighboring school district consolidated and received a grant. Supervised by the Department of Education, they built a new school building and began bringing rural schoolchildren to school in horse-drawn vans. In 1914 a model of the school became part of an exhibit at the San Francisco Exposition of that year. In 1917 Alberta High School had its first graduates.

Photo – Alberta, Mn Consolidated School c. 1941

A generally recognized obstacle to school consolidation was the reluctance of well-educated teachers to come to small towns or rural areas, which usually had no place for them to live or eat. George E. Vincent, the president of the University of Minnesota, was interested in school consolidation as an answer to this problem. He persuaded the Rockefeller Foundation to contribute $3,000 (half the cost) to the Alberta school to build a residence for the teachers. That was a lot of money for a poor little hamlet like Alberta with about thirty families. In 1916, after heated debate, the voters approved the building, 72-63. "The Manse," as it was known, was completed in 1917 and dedicated by the state superintendent of education.

The school building burned in 1931, although the Manse was saved. By that time the rural roads had been much improved, and students were coming by school bus. The gleaming new building was opened in 1932; it was only three years old when Clayton and I enrolled there. The state Department of Education sent a dynamic superintendent, Mr. J. H. Kerlan, to run the school. Mother told me that Kerlan was expected to return to the department after gaining experience with school consolidation in Alberta. Mr. Kerlan's stay in Alberta (1934-42) coincided almost exactly with the years that we were there, after which he returned to his reward in St. Paul.

Mr. Kerlan was a remarkable man. He was short, energetic, bright-eyed, enthusiastic, and assertive, with a quick temper and a quick smile. He had lost his right arm, but he used the stump effectively. He was athletic and liked to display his facility in sports, despite his handicap. When playing baseball he would catch the ball in his glove, toss the ball in the air, deftly put the glove under his stump, catch the ball, and throw it back. He could shoot a basketball reasonably well too, using his stump as a hand.

Kerlan recruited excellent young teachers from the University of Minnesota or from good teachers colleges such as St. Cloud and Mankato. Salaries could not have been very good, but teachers would come to a dismal little town like Alberta because the school was excellent and the Manse provided attractive and economical housing. One teacher described the Manse as "like living in a sorority house." The teachers operated this establishment as a co-op, with a cook-housekeeper. The Kerlans had the downstairs of the Manse for their housing.

Moving from a rural school in Bay City to the Alberta Consolidated School was one of several fortunate events (another was the GI Bill) that made it possible for me to get a good education and pursue a professional career. But before I could benefit from the advantages of a good school I had a great adjustment to make. In Bay City I was a smart little kid; in Alberta I discovered how far behind I was.

My first day is burned into my memory as one of the greatest shocks of my life, comparable in its impact to my first day of combat in World War II. We moved in February, 1935, and thus I had the problem of entering in the middle of the school year. Dad walked Clayton and me to school (Phil was still too young) and took us to our rooms, where he met our teachers. We were nicely dressed in new navy-blue corduroy pants. When we arrived I was impressed and awed by the large, imposing building with its broad, shining corridors.

My room had the fifth and sixth grades. I was in the fifth grade (Miss Paulson) and Clayton was in the third grade (Miss Kespohl). There were two closets at the back of the room where Miss Paulson told me to hang my cap and coat. I did so and sat down at the desk she pointed out. It was quiet, because we were early and the other children had not yet arrived. I think she asked me a few questions and probably checked my reading skills, which of course were good. I know I was anxious, as any child would be in a new school, but school was my special talent so I suppose I felt reasonably confident.

Soon the other children began arriving, most of them rough and boisterous, red-faced from the cold, slamming closet doors, banging desks, and jabbering away despite Miss Paulson's hard-nosed efforts (she was indeed hard-nosed) to bring these semibarbarians into order.

My first humiliation was to notice that unwittingly I had hung my coat in the girl's closet, an unpardonable offense. The greatest humiliation of all was to discover that I did not know what was going on. A feeling swept over me of total humiliation, rage, and loneliness. It was traumatic. Tears rolled down my cheeks. When we went out for recess I was immediately set upon by older boys applying the bullying techniques of the school yard on this new kid, who was small, anxious, and obviously vulnerable. They also spotted Clayton and brought him over, questioning which of us was the better fighter.

In no time at all we were wrestling furiously on the ground, getting our new corduroy pants covered with dust. Miss Paulson came rushing out, eyes blazing, and parted us. She did not scold or punish me, which would have been the ultimate personal shock, but she took us back into the school and dusted us off. When I walked home for dinner one of the kids in my class walked along with me showing some commiseration. My Mother undoubtedly saw that I had had a bad time of it, but she did not inquire too much. I must put that day down as one of the worst of my life.

Of course I eventually adjusted to my new school and my academic ability put me among the best in the class, although there were other good students too. I was strong in history, geography, and reading, and less able in arithmetic. We had plenty of schoolbooks and other necessary equipment. I enjoyed poring over the maps in my geography book, looking at the products and crops in different parts of the world. From my history books I learned about explorers, colonists, Indians, presidents, and heroes. I learned that America was "the land of the free and the home of the brave" and had never lost a war. We began every day with the Pledge of Allegiance. I learned to sight-read music using syllables, and I still do that today.

Under Mr. Kerlan's leadership the school had adopted an idea that was new at the time: junior high. When I advanced into seventh grade I moved upstairs and became part of Alberta High School. The seventh and eighth graders had their own home room, but they followed the high school pattern in that they attended classes in special subjects with different teachers. In the back of our home room was a library room with large glass windows so that the home room teacher could look into it. I recall a pretty good collection of reference works and books, so that we could really do class reports.

In the ninth grade Alberta High School had an infusion of students when the first group of ninth graders came from Donnelly, a small town about nine miles north of Alberta. I remember the excitement the day we first met our new classmates. The Donnelly kids were a good-looking, lively bunch, but all the best students in the class were from Alberta.

We had good teachers, who insisted that we pay attention and do our work. My strongest suits were history, geography, and literature. I had to work hard in math, geometry, and physics. I did not take biology because I did not want to cut up a frog. We had a surprising number of school activities, such as the school newspaper, plays, musical groups and the like. Disrespect was unheard of, and if it occurred Mr. Kerlan would mete out swift punishment, to say nothing of what would happen to the offender at home. Attendance was not a problem, except if kept home by farm work or snow, since there was no place else to go.

High school was not a happy time for me, as is often the case in adolescence. I was small and personally immature – the smart little kid with glasses. Due to skipping the second grade, I was a year younger than my classmates, an important consideration at that age. I was accepted by my classmates, but I never felt like one of them. They were were good-natured small town/rural young people, without pretensions or snobbism, who came to school expecting to do their assignments and have some fun too. Their misdeeds were limited to such mild offenses as whispering, chewing gum, or passing notes. By the time we graduated some pairs were forming, which frequently meant that after graduation they would get married and settle down.

Sports were an important activity at Alberta High School, but I did not participate. Apart from my small size, organized sports were not part of my family's experience. Before we moved to Alberta I had never seen a game of football or basketball, or an organized game of baseball. However, I did become the student manager and travelled with the team, looking after balls and uniforms.

Alberta High School had a fine new building but it did not have a gym, which says something about educational values in those days. Basketball games were a major event for everyone in the town. The basketball team played in the town hall, a rectangular building with a floor just barely adequate for basketball. The students sat on the stage and the players and adults sat on chairs along the side walls. In those days, basketball was a slow-moving game emphasizing floor movement and passing to get a layup. When that failed, one of the guards would try a two-handed set shot. The jump shot had not been invented, fast breaks were rare, and the dunk was unknown.

In 1940 Alberta began six-man football. I knew about football from the papers and listening to radio broadcasts of the Minnesota Gophers, but I had never seen a game, apart from pickup games in the park. The first year our team lacked finesse, but we had some big players and won all our games until our boys lost the last game – and the championship – to Chokio, the next town to the west. During the Depression, six-man football was ideal for small schools that had neither the players nor the money for the eleven-man game.

The Tap Team

Closely tied in with athletics was the Alberta High School Tap Team, organized by Mrs. Kerlan, a bright-eyed, lively young woman who taught tap-dancing. These were the most attractive girls in school, dolled up in cute costumes that Mrs. Kerlan sewed. Piano accompaniment was provided by Miss Beardsley, an elementary grade teacher. The Tap Team performed at all home basketball games and was in great demand for away games, where they were understandably popular.

Mrs. Kerlan got the idea that I should be their announcer, with top hat and cane, introducing each number in my bright, piping voice. One day the Tap Team made a tour of three high schools in the area, where they performed for the high school assemblies. There was a break in the action when they changed costumes, and I decided to fill the time by telling a few jokes. I got a good response, and that became part of the routine.

My role as Tap Team announcer led to one of the highlights of my high school days. The Tap Team was invited to perform at half-time at the Minnesota state basketball tournament, where I introduced them over a loudspeaker. After that we performed at the Minnesota Room of the Hotel Nicollet, the most elegant nightclub in the Twin Cities. When the band leader handed me the microphone, I cracked a few jokes. These went over very well with the customers, who were surprised at seeing this poised little fellow with his troupe of pretty high school girls.

Afterwards we had club sandwiches and cokes at a table on a raised area at the back. The Minnesota Room had a first-rate band led by a man who went by the name of Ran Wilde. The band was so elegant that it even had two violins. Some of the girls wanted to get out on the dance floor, but Mrs. Kerlan would not let them dance with each other, as they often did at home. I was the only possible partner, and I never went to dances and did not know how to dance. I cringed at this demonstration of my evident inadequacy. Ah, the agonies of high school!

Back to the Violin

I was a senior in high school when I decided I wanted to resume playing the violin. Dad found a music teacher in Morris who had played the violin at one time. He agreed to take me on, although he did not normally give private lessons. This music teacher, whose name I have forgotten, was a genial man about sixty years of age. He was a competent musician and a pleasant but undemanding teacher. One evening a week during that school year Dad would drive me to Morris and wait in the car while I had my lesson. It says something about the constraints under which I lived that Dad would not consider my making this simple drive myself, even though I had my driver's license.

I became quite dedicated and practiced regularly, although I cannot say that I made much progress. Then, as now, I had interest but not an exceptional talent. At school I got permission to practice in the laundry room of the Manse during my home room period. Occasionally Mrs. Kerlan would enter apologetically to put in another load of wash. For a while playing the violin was associated in my mind with the odor of soap, bluing, and wet clothes.

Church

Trinity Lutheran Church was a congregation of the Norwegian Lutheran Church. The church building was a handsome example of the type, with a dramatic altar painting of Christ walking on the water. The church basement was used for Sunday school, and was also the setting for the hot-dish dinners offered by the Ladies Aid society three or four times a year. Mom put more meat in her hot-dish than some of the others, so hers always went quickly. She would not stoop to that inexpensive Depression staple, macaroni and cheese, as some ladies did.

Alberta also had a small Nazarene congregation which occupied a covered basement until money became available to complete the building. Once, when there was a revival going on, Mother and I attended at the invitation of a member. The worship was much too overheated for us. Alberta also had a fair number of Catholics who drove to Morris for mass. One time I stopped briefly in the home of a Catholic family next door and saw a crucifix on the wall. Having grown up with sulphurous Old Testament injunctions against idols and graven images, it made me feel very uncomfortable.

Photo – Alberta, Mn – Trinity Lutheran Church 1980s

The Norwegian Lutheran Church had brought from Norway the tradition of a learned clergy, trained in the Bible (including the study of Hebrew and Greek) and thoroughly imbued with the doctrines of the Reformation. The worship was dignified, sermons were carefully prepared, the hymns had musical merit, and the tone of Sunday worship varied from sedate to mildly boring. I took church seriously, and the church fostered my scholarly inclinations. When I graduated from high school I had read all of the New Testament and much of the Old.

Our pastor for most of the time that we lived in Alberta was Rev. C. Arthur Olsen. He was not a stimulating preacher nor a smooth conversationalist, but he was a fine exemplar of the Lutheran scholarly tradition. He had a powerful singing voice that rang out as he sang the liturgy and led the congregational singing. When I conversed with him many years later, he told me that, since his ordination, he had made it his practice to study his Greek New Testament every day.

Of course, we attended church services and Sunday school regularly. We always sat in the same place, as did most people. Mother sang in the choir. Our church had the usual Christmas festivities and Sunday school program. Contrasting with the joy of

Christmas was the dismal season of Lent, when the sermons dealt much with sin, reinforced by ponderous German hymns that dragged on through many verses expressing sentiments of abject penitence. The doleful message of Lent was reinforced by the dreariness of our protracted winter, until Easter and spring brought blessed relief.

A major step in my religious life was confirmation, for which it was necessary to prepare by one year of catechism classes meeting on Saturday mornings. I memorized the long catechism with its many questions and answers and Bible passages that supported its teachings. Every Friday evening, Dad required me to recite the material to him to show that I was prepared for catechism class on Saturday morning. In so doing, a rudimentary theological system was implanted in my mind before I realized what was happening.

The night before I was confirmed Dad asked me to meet him at his office in the bank. He gave me my confirmation Bible (which I still have) with a typed note in it. Apparently he thought it was his duty to give me some good advice at this significant point in my life. I don't recall what he said, but I know I was moved by the opportunity for a personal father-son talk.

Phil has the best account of Dad's performance of his paternal duty.

"Phil," Dad said, "when you go through life you will meet lots of people who want you to do things you shouldn't do."

"Well," he concluded emphatically, "don't do 'em."

I imagine that he gave me similar advice.

My confirmation day was an emotional experience for me. That evening we had communion. I felt proud to kneel at the altar rail with my Dad and Mom as an adult, at least in the eyes of God and the Church.

Activities

Dad liked Alberta because of the great pheasant hunting. He was a crack shot. More than once he was out at dawn and back with his limit in time to open the bank. He had great physical stamina in his forties and early fifties, just as I did at that age, and he could keep hunting all day if necessary to get his limit. We boys served as his bird dogs, going ahead to flush out the pheasants and retrieving them when they fell. When I follow my ball down the fairway in pursuit of a different kind of "birdie," I remember how Dad would hustle to get a pheasant that he had knocked down. Dad's hunting was his principal recreation, but it also had economic value by providing meat in those hard times. Sometimes we boys got so tired of eating pheasant that we would plead for hamburger or a ring of bologna.

When I was about sixteen I got a 20-gauge shotgun. I remember the first day that I went hunting with Dad. I was on one side of a ravine and he was on the other. A pheasant flushed up and flew down the ravine. We both fired. Dad insisted that I had shot the pheasant, but when we cleaned it the bird shot was all on his side. I never became very good at shooting birds on the fly.

One day Dad came home with a .22 rifle from Bill Braun's. He said he was just going to try it out, but from the scowl on Mom's face I knew he would buy it. We boys were thrilled. On Sunday afternoons we would walk along the tracks and shoot at gophers or at a tin can set on a fencepost. I learned to handle a rifle quite well. In the army I became a rifleman and earned a sharpshooter medal.

Dad also liked fishing. In the summer we would go fishing at Lake Minnewaska, a large lake at Starbuck. Dad was as unsuccessful in fishing as he was successful in hunting. This lack of success stifled any interest that I might have developed in the sport. We did not know the lake: we just rowed out to what seemed a likely spot, usually because other people were fishing there, dropped anchor, and fished from the side of the boat. At times we trolled for pike, but we did not have a motor and could not afford to rent one, so trolling meant tedious rowing.

I was about twelve years old when I got a bicycle. Mainly I rode it around town. One Saturday morning I decided to ride my bike to Morris and take in a movie. The sky was gray and the wind was from the east, which made it hard going, but I got there. When I rode home the wind was at my back and there was a beautiful sunset ahead of me. It was a glorious feeling. I don't know why I didn't do that more often, but I did it only once.

The annual trips to Grove City continued. We purred along the highway at thirty-five miles an hour in our square 1928 Chevy with solid wheels while newer, faster, streamlined cars passed us. The tires went bump-bump-bump on the expansion joints that separated the concrete slabs. After Morris we proceeded through a boring sequence of little towns: Hancock, Clontarf, Benson, DeGraff, Murdock, Pennock, and Kerkhoven. Each had its distinctive water tower rising through the trees, and we played a game to see who could spot it first. When we reached Willmar, the only town of any size, we knew we were getting close. Our first stop was usually "Auntwater."

A sign of our increasing prosperity (perhaps declining poverty would be a better expression) came in 1940 when Dad bought a new Chevrolet with the shift lever on the steering column. By that time I was old enough to get a driver's license, and Dad undertook to teach me to drive. He was a terrible teacher: I learned to shift and steer, but he taught me nothing about the rules of the road. He really didn't want me driving his fine new car at all. Mom and Dad let me drive only when I was with them, and they were so anxious about it I decided it wasn't worth the hassle. I did not learn to drive until after the war when I got my own car, and then I taught myself.

Our house was not far from the town park, where the Alberta boys played pickup games of baseball and football. There wasn't much else for town kids to do. The boys in Alberta all had gloves, and there were enough bats and baseballs (sometimes wound with black tape) to serve the purpose. Sometimes we played touch football, and sometimes we tackled. When "the dinky" came through town at 5:30 P.M. it was time to go home for supper.

Apart from the school, Alberta had no facilities for basketball, and nobody that I knew owned a basketball. People did not have paved driveways, and the basket over the driveway, today the universal sign of a boy in the house, had not yet appeared.

The most surprising omission was the lack of a skating rink. In Alberta, recreation was not given much consideration. People's lives (especially farm people) were filled with work. Little or no value was attached to play, for children or anyone else. A skating rink was not the kind of facility that people in Alberta would think of, nor did the town have city water to flood one. Thus, we grew up in that frozen northland at a time of long, cold winters, and we did not learn to skate or play hockey.

Amateur baseball was well organized in Minnesota, and many small towns had their town teams. These teams were comprised of local young men and any good players who could be persuaded to come from a distance. In the summertime, the Sunday afternoon baseball game was a great event for people who had very little entertainment.

The Alberta team was managed by Jack Schultz, the grocer. Several of his sons played on the team: Lee Schultz was at first base, Bud Schultz at shortstop, and Julian, "Spike" Schultz (Julene's twin) played center field. Bob Treischel, owner of the cafe, who was a judicious, level-headed man, was the local umpire. Since he was the only umpire, he called balls and strikes (and everything else) from the mound, behind the pitcher.

Alberta had a great year when Jack Schultz recruited the pitcher and catcher of the University of Minnesota baseball team. They drove up from the Twin Cities every Sunday to play for Alberta. I was told they got twenty dollars per game, but it might have been more. I can still hear Treischel call out: "Battery for Alberta: Remington and Reimers. Play ball." (Cheers from the crowd, who were confident they would get a well-pitched game.)

With this outside help, Alberta won most of its scheduled games and went to the state amateur tournament. Nothing like that had ever happened in Alberta before. The level of enthusiasm and anxiety was enormous. In the first round the team lost a heartbreaker to Delano, and gloom hung over the town for days. Delano is on U.S. 12 between the Twin Cities, Grove City, and points west. On my many trips from Illinois to Minnesota over the years, every time I drove through Delano I relived the pain.

Since we enjoyed the games, Mom got some white flannel and blue piping and made us baseball uniforms like those the team wore. When we appeared at the ballpark we were a great hit with the spectators. Out of spite and envy, however, some young ruffians called out: "What's that you're wearing, your pajamas?" I was extremely indignant that anyone would call my baseball uniform pajamas. Honesty compels me to admit that when winter came my Mother was not about to see good flannel go to waste, and we wore them as pajamas after all.

The Media

Until I went to college I never lived in a town with a public library or a movie theatre. Our Saturday afternoon trips to Morris provided access to those two valuable institutional supports for immigrant families crossing the bridge. Mom always stopped at the library, and by the time we left Alberta little Norma could join her three brothers in checking out books. It is not surprising that eventually she became a librarian.

I was a constant reader, partly because I enjoyed it and partly because in Alberta there wasn't much else to do. I liked "Treasure Island" and other books of adventure. I early discovered the Tarzan books by Edgar Rice Burroughs and read as many as I could get my hands on. I read Zane Grey's "Riders of the Purple Sage", but I did not become a fan of his cowboy books, although they were enormously popular in those days. I liked books about the sea, probably because we lived so far from it. In high school I read C. S. Forester's books about Horatio Hornblower and the Nordhoff and Hall books about the South Sea islands ("Mutiny on the Bounty", "Men Against the Sea", and "Pitcairn's Island"). Like everybody else, I read "Gone with the Wind" when it came out. Fiction with a religious basis attracted me, especially Lew Wallace, "Ben Hur" and Lloyd Douglas, "The Robe", written by a Lutheran clergyman. Another favorite was James Hilton's "Lost Horizon". Somehow I happened upon the English version of Ernst Renan's "Life of Jesus" (1888), a romantic work that portrayed Jesus as a good and kindly moral teacher but not the son of God. The book did not shake my faith, as it had for many in its day, but it gave me a sense of another dimension to the Gospel story. Our school library had J. B. Priestley's "The Good Companions", which I enjoyed very much. Closer to home was Sinclair Lewis' "Main Street", based on his life in Sauk Centre, Minnesota. Lewis was something of a black sheep in our parts, since "Main Street" was a satirical treatment of small-town Minnesota life. In short, I was reading the books that were popular with mainstream America, and my mind was being enlarged beyond the narrow boundaries of Alberta and my Norwegian-American heritage.

I read things that were more substantial too. By the time I went to college I had read much of the Bible and many of Shakespeare's plays. I liked Daniel Defoe's "Robinson Crusoe". Being something of an outsider myself, I took satisfaction in Crusoe's ability to survive on his own, although conveniently provided with a shipload of tools and supplies. Dickens' "David Copperfield", with its resilient hero helped along life's road by many good people, reassured me that my family and I could cope with our ups and downs.

The popular media were important in helping immigrant populations cross the bridge to mainstream America, and I was very susceptible to their attractions. Throughout my entire life the newspaper has been the foundation of all my reading. Dad continued to subscribe to the Minneapolis *Journal*, which came a day later by mail. He would pick it up in the post office early in the morning and read it before he opened the bank. As time went on, I became more interested in the news. I also discovered Dorothea Dix's column of advice to lovers and spouses; I was growing up.

The comic strips continued to be a source of information as well as entertainment. I remember when "Dick Tracy" began and when "Superman" first appeared. I shudder to think how much of my stock of indiscriminate knowledge may go back originally to comic strips. Although other kids had comic books (which they read surreptitiously in study hall), Mom would not let us buy them. She said they were a waste of money. I suspect she thought they would have bad moral effects.

I read the sports pages too, where I followed the Minneapolis Millers and St. Paul Saints of the American Association and the Golden Gophers of the Big Ten. I did not follow major league baseball, although I knew about stars like Dizzy Dean, Joe Medwick, Gabby Hartnett, Lou Gehrig, Mickey Cochrane, Bob Feller, Hank Greenberg, Joe Dimaggio, and Ted Williams. I had a large collection of pictures of prominent athletes clipped from the sports pages. Dad and Mom liked to go to local games, but they did not follow professional sports.

We had few magazine subscriptions. We took *McCalls* for Mom and *Boy's Life* for me and my brothers. We also received the *Lutheran Herald*, the magazine of our church. We could not afford those middle-class favorites, *Reader's Digest* and the *Saturday Evening Post*. Nor did we take *Time* or *Life*, which by 1940 had become the most influential magazines in America.

The American entertainment industry was another major factor in the assimilation of immigrant populations. The movies took us to a world of glamour, wit, sophistication, and adventure. We did not go often, but our Saturday afternoon shopping trips to Morris sometimes included a matinee. I especially liked Mickey Rooney/Judy Garland movies, and I recall the tremendous lift I got from the jazz in "Birth of the Blues". We did not go to "Gone with the Wind", for which higher prices were charged. For the same reason, we did not see "Snow White and the Seven Dwarfs".

Travelling shows, usually performed in a tent or the town hall, were the small-town/rural equivalent of vaudeville. In western Minnesota the best known was Christy Obrecht, whose omnipresent signs were posted on telephone poles. To moralists like my Mother these shows were suspect, mainly due to their racy jokes. Our corner of the state had a troupe called Johnny Campbell. For several winters the Johnny Campbell Players (five men, five women) came to the Alberta town hall one night a week for about eight weeks. On other nights they played at the other little towns along our highway (Minnesota 28). The tickets were inexpensive, and almost everybody went to Johnny Campbell.

The show began with a play, either a comedy or a mystery. It concluded with a dance (the actors all played musical instruments too). One season my Uncle Carl Jensen turned up as the accordion player. Uncle Carl, who was very shy, couldn't act, but they needed a good man on the accordion and he fit the bill. He also earned his keep by putting up scenery, loading luggage, driving the bus, and serving as general handyman.

The main source of Depression-era entertainment was the radio. Every Sunday night we listened to Jack Benny and Fred Allen. We especially enjoyed their famous feud, where Allen was the clear winner although Benny had the larger audience. Tuesday night was Edgar Bergen and Charlie McCarthy and Bob Hope. This was the age of the big bands, which were featured on Saturday night. The highlight of Saturday night was "The Hit Parade", featuring Frank Sinatra. There was always interest in school as to which song would be No. 1.

Probably the most important program of the week came on Monday nights: "Lux Radio Theater", which presented one-hour adaptations of current movies. "Did you hear Lux last night?" was a common question in school on Tuesday morning. "Lux" featured famous actors and actresses, like Clark Gable or Bette Davis, who were introduced by Cecil B. DeMille, the famous director of cinematic spectacles. We did not go to the movies very often, so "Lux" was the next best thing.

In my senior year I began listening to the Sunday afternoon broadcasts of the New York Philharmonic Orchestra. There I heard the famous violinists of the day. I was thrilled when the Beethoven violin concerto was performed, the theme of which I had learned when I was taking lessons in Bay City. I also recall a time when the violins opened the concert by playing in unison the familiar Kreutzer violin etude, No. 2. Everyone – the announcer, the musicians, and the audience – thought it was a delightful novelty.

Our clearest station was WDAY, Fargo. At noon they had a program called "Dinner Bell Time" that featured Old Time music. I recall a day on "Dinner Bell Time" when the announcer introduced a new singer. He stated effusively that they expected great things from MISS PEGGY LEE! This incident sticks in my mind, because I had become sophisticated enough to scorn the idea that anyone from "Dinner Bell Time" could ever amount to anything. Eventually Peggy Lee became one of the great vocalists of my generation: the female equivalent of Frank Sinatra. Similarly, I never anticipated the success of Lawrence Welk, who played dances and county fairs in our area and whose signs were seen from time to time on telephone poles.

Another memorable aspect of radio was sports broadcasting. In the summer I listened to the Minneapolis Millers of the American Association. In the autumn we had broadcasts of Bernie Bierman's Minnesota Gophers, where I first learned to recognize the names of colleges and universities. Most exciting of all were the heavyweight fights, announced by the super-dramatic Clem McCarthy. The broadcasts were sponsored by Gillette blue blades. In these days, when beer is the pre-eminent advertiser, it is hard to realize that before World War II sports were sponsored by makers of razor blades and Wheaties.

Boxing was dominated by the march of Joe Louis to the heavyweight crown. In the summertime, Bill Braun would hook up a loudspeaker at his gas station/garage and people would sit on the curb to listen to the fight. Among the older people there was considerable resistance to "the nigger," but from the beginning I was a fan of "the brown bomber." It broke my heart when he lost to Max Schmeling, the German, but his victory in a rematch was some consolation.

Love

It is customary in memoirs of this kind to say something about the young man's awakening to romantic love. My words on this topic will be few. Apart from the reticence on such matters typical of my family, another reason for brevity is the lack of anything interesting to report. Being impressionable and sensitive, I was attracted by the charms of what in those days was known as "the fair sex." But I was terribly ill at ease with all girls, and especially those that interested me.

To me, girls were creatures from another world. I grew up in a household which was all-male except for my mother and baby sister, who were not envisaged in gendered terms. In those days society in rural Minnesota was a male bastion: men ran the show and women did their duties. Furthermore, in my teenage days we were not drenched in sexuality, like today. Most of what I knew about sex came from watching animals on the farm. Instead of "sex" we had "LOVE," that tender emotion idealized by poets and novelists to which book-readers, like myself, were especially susceptible.

In Mickey Rooney-Judy Garland movies I saw the kind of relationship with a girl that I wanted, but such was not for me. Dating required a car, and I did not drive our car except with my parents. We did not even have a telephone. There was no "girl next door" with whom I might walk to school or spend an idle hour. I was not permitted to go to dances, and young people did not have house parties. The only thing to do on a date was to go to Morris to the movies, which meant asking for the car and arousing more anxieties, in addition to getting up the nerve to ask the girl in the first place.

Painful as it is, I must tell about my one effort to break the established mold and have a party. I knew about parties from books and movies. Mom, who was sensitive to these things, thought it would be better for young people to have parties instead of going to dances and roaring around in cars on Saturday nights. When I said that some evening I would like to have a party for the cast of the class play after rehearsal, she willingly agreed and made goodies and decorations. Since a party was an unaccustomed thing in Alberta, I felt very proud of myself. Miss Aamodt (the play director) and the students were quite pleased at the idea of coming to our house.

What happened was a disaster. Dad, who didn't understand what this was all about, perched himself in the living room, baby Norma on his lap, and carried on a conversation with Miss Aamodt, while the students sat and fidgeted. Realizing that my party had become a terrible bore, I burned with indignation and humiliation, hoping that Dad would leave the room, but he just sat there enjoying himself. Finally everybody had something to eat and went home and that was it.

Dad loused up my one and only party, but at this distance I don't blame him. He was head of the household, and when people came to his house he expected to be present. My idea of a teenage party came from books and movies, which were not part of his world. I knew then there was no use fighting it; when I left home I could do things my way.

Politics

We Reitans were unusual in Alberta in that we were Republicans. As the town banker, Dad probably thought that being a Republican was a necessary part of his profession. Mother was a Republican because the Republicans had established Prohibition and Roosevelt had brought back beer. She associated Republicans with respectability and middle-class morality, while the Democrats seemed to appeal to people who drank and were unwilling to work and scrimp as we did. We boys were Republicans because our parents were.

Most people in Alberta were Democrats because they were poor and the Democrats helped the poor. The farmers depended on New Deal farm programs for survival, and the town depended on the farmers. New Deal "make-work" programs provided for the unemployed. Minnesota in the 1930s had a strong tradition of prairie populism, led by Gov. Floyd B. Olson and the Farmer-Labor Party. They were very much opposed to bankers, railroads, grain dealers, meat-packing companies, and other businesses that were said to grind the faces of the poor. On the national level the Farmer-Labor Party supported the Democratic candidates, and eventually they merged with the Democratic Party. Whatever their political affiliations, people in Alberta all had a kind of basic patriotism that respected the laws, symbols, and heroes of our country.

Our next-door neighbors, the Spauldings, were among the few other Republicans in town. In 1936 Mrs. Spaulding paid me fifty cents to deliver literature for the Republican presidential candidates, Landon and Knox, who lost to Roosevelt in a landslide. Despite my parents' Republicanism, when I got into high school and began learning more about public affairs, my views began to change. I came to respect Roosevelt's efforts to use the powers of the federal government to lead the country out of the Depression. And I began to understand the concern of the Roosevelt administration with the growing threat of war abroad.

In the summer of 1940 I listened on the radio to the exciting Republican national convention that nominated Wendell Willkie. Calling the roll of the states was a dramatic ritual, made even more interesting by the varied accents of the delegates. I was thrilled by Willkie's dramatic nomination, but by then I was accustomed to Roosevelt as president and was on my way to becoming a Democrat.

War

By the time I was in high school, international tensions had become cause for concern. The Minneapolis *Journal* was Republican and isolationist, but radio news broadcasts were more alarmist. The networks offered fifteen-minute evening newscasts presented by commentators such H. V. Kaltenborn, Boak Carter, and Gabriel Heatter. At the movies, newsreels brought German and Japanese militarism vividly to our attention. The Lutheran churches, whose missionaries had long been active in China, called attention to Japanese depredations there. My awareness of China was enhanced when I read Pearl Buck's "The Good Earth", a sympathetic and touching novel of Chinese life written by an offspring of missionaries. We probably saw the movie too, which won an Academy Award.

In September 1939 war broke out in Europe, when Hitler and Stalin attacked Poland. The war seemed remote at the time, but it was something interesting to follow in the news. Dad was a typical

Midwestern isolationist until April 1940, when Hitler over-ran Norway and Denmark. Then he became an angry interventionist, probably not thinking that some day one or more of his sons might become involved in the fighting. Mom didn't like the idea of war – period – and she thought that we should stay out of it, despite any sympathies she might have felt for Hitler's victims.

In June and July 1940 France fell and Britain struggled desperately to survive. When the German bombing of London began, the radio broadcasts of Edward R. Murrow brought the war into our living room in a way that the newspaper never could. Mr. Kerlan was a great admirer of Churchill. When Churchill made one of his famous "do or die" broadcasts, Mr. Kerlan brought all the high school students and teachers into the study hall, turned on a short-wave radio, and we listened to the speech. I couldn't understand any of it: Churchill's accent was hard enough to follow and the reception was poor. However, this experience impressed on me that important things were happening overseas that might affect America some time.

As President Roosevelt called upon Americans to aid Britain, the interventionist-isolationist debate became the great issue in Middle America. The Selective Service System was established and registration began. The Alberta draft board used the Cargill grain elevator for registration, and I was employed on several Saturdays to type up the information. The idea that I would some day be drafted was perhaps in my mind, but it seemed unreal.

Soon the draft began to hit home. News came that this one had been drafted, or that the draft had gotten that one. The big ears of little Norma, at that time four years old, took in this news at the dinner table.

One cold winter day Norma was playing by the leaky back door. "Norma," Mom said, "come here. There's a draft back there."

Norma screamed in fright as she dashed into the kitchen. She didn't know what kind of a monster a draft was, but she didn't want it to get her.

December 7, 1941 was a typical cold, gray, dreary winter Sunday in Minnesota. I suppose we went to church in the morning and ate the usual big Sunday dinner. I was looking forward to the Sunday evening radio programs. That afternoon the radio began broadcasting the news that the Japanese had attacked Pearl Harbor in the Hawaiian Islands. We were at war!

Of course there was much excitement that evening, as the scheduled programs were interrupted for additional bulletins. The next morning Mr. Kerlan called an assembly to discuss what had happened. My classmates and I were seniors, and it began to sink in that the war would soon have an effect on our lives. After Dad's pugnacity and anger had worn off, I could see that both my parents were very worried.

Disaster Strikes

It was in February 1942 that an unexpected blow fell. I recall a morning when Dad did not go to the bank as usual. He seemed quite excited. He put on a fresh white shirt, his best suit and tie, set his brown fedora on his head, got in the car and left. There was a sense of mystery in the air. After he left Mom said that we might be moving to Morris. I was thrilled. By my standards, Morris was a real city.

When Dad returned at noon for dinner, he put a good face on the bad news. He had lost his job. The war had stimulated the economy and farm prices were up. By working very hard Dad had made the bank profitable. A bank in Morris had bought the Alberta State Bank and intended to transfer the accounts to Morris. They had no interest in keeping the bank open or employing Dad. We were left high and dry.

There were four shareholders, including Schultz and Larson. Why would they sell a bank (small as it was) that was profitable and brought customers to town? My guess is that they were dominated by the Depression mentality and decided to sell out while the getting was good. They received something over $40,000 for the bank. Split four ways, that was a nice chunk of money in those days. Larson may have resented Dad's wrangles with Lucille. Schultz wanted to keep the bank, but apparently he had no choice but to go along with Larson and the other two shareholders. Eventually the bank building was converted into a bar, an ironic twist of fate considering my parents' opposition to strong drink.

In the mid-1950s, on one of my trips from Illinois, I stopped in Alberta and conversed with Lee Schultz, who had succeeded his father in the store. "Selling the bank was the dumbest thing we could have done," he said. "When people had to go to Morris to do their banking, they stayed to do their shopping. There is nothing left here." I found scant consolation in that admission.

Dad, at age fifty, without a high school diploma, was again looking for a job. He had lost his job in Grove City because the bank lost money. He lost his job in Alberta because the bank made money. How unlucky can anyone be?

In the meantime I was a senior, preparing to graduate from Alberta High School and go on to Concordia College in Moorhead, Minnesota, the nearest college of our church. One bitterly cold winter night we boys slept in the living room because it was too cold upstairs. As a result of this circumstance, I overheard Mom and Dad talking in the bedroom about their plight.

Dad was totally discouraged.

"Who will want me at my age?" he asked.

Mom insisted that he would find something. Then she brought up the subject of sending Earl to college.

"We have got to send Earl for the first year," she said. "If he goes for one year he will find ways to finish," she added, "but if he doesn't go the first year he will probably never go at all."

"And if Earl goes to college," she concluded, "the others will too."

How many children are ever privy to their parents' confidential conversations, and on a matter so important to their own future? I realized that I had heard and learned something very important. I vowed that I would not let my parents down. Then I wept into my pillow. At that moment I was set in the direction that has shaped the rest of my life.

While the Alberta State Bank was being sold, the "Leave the Building Alone" found its final solution. A farm couple named Kampmeyer decided to retire and move to town. They offered to buy the house for $2,000. Dad, true to the principles of good business, agreed that the house should be sold and the moribund building and loan terminated. The deal was made, and we had to move.

Where would we live? Under the circumstances, we needed only temporary housing. The cream station next to the bank, from which we had borrowed milk cans, had been closed. The owner had remodeled it into a dwelling of minimal standards. So we moved into the cream station, hoping that something would turn up soon.

Graduation

Such were the unfortunate circumstances of our family in May 1942 when I graduated from Alberta High School. As salutatorian of the class I was required to give a formal address at commencement. In typical teenage fashion I had forgotten to do anything about it until the last minute. Shortly before graduation day, Mr. Kerlan informed me that he was submitting the program to the printer and needed to know the title of my talk right away. I had to act quickly.

Looking for a theme, I began paging through my English literature book. I came upon Tennyson's "Locksley Hall" which includes the lines:

> *For I dipped into the future,*
> *Far as human eye could see.*
> *Saw the Vision of the world,*
> *And all the wonders that would be.*

This seemed like a good theme for commencement, so I entitled my address "A Dip into the Future." Then I had to get busy and write it. My talk was filled with optimistic hogwash about opportunities and progress, little heeding that there was a war going on and that my personal and family future looked grim.

Finally graduation day arrived. Mom and Dad had not graduated from high school, and they were determined that all the niceties of graduation would be observed. I wore a cap and gown and delivered my address. Mom put on a nice party in the cream station. Aunt Rose and Uncle Ben came from Atwater for the occasion. Rose could not avoid bemoaning the misfortune that had befallen us. "Oh, Earnest," she sobbed, "you should have stayed on the farm."

Dad seemed to agree.

Regent

Eventually something did turn up. Dad got a job in a small bank in Regent, North Dakota, in the far southwestern part of the state. Unlike the paupers of Bay City, the solid citizens of Alberta did not give us a party or a gift, although we had been respected, contributing citizens of the town for seven years. Perhaps they were too embarrassed and ashamed at what had happened to us. Our last Sunday in church Rev. Olson, of course, bid us farewell, and after the service members of the congregation came to express their best wishes for the future. I think even L. M. Larson and Mrs. Larson felt obligated to say something.

Once again we quietly folded our tents and slipped away. In mid-August a truck pulled up at our house, the well-worn Grove City furniture was loaded, and we set off for western North Dakota via Fargo-Moorhead, Valley City, Jamestown, and Bismarck. In our new car, the miles slipped quickly behind us. At Mandan we crossed the Missouri River, and after that the car worked harder as it climbed the high plains. At Dickinson, not far from the Montana border, we took a secondary road southward into a rolling landscape punctuated with buttes that rose dramatically out of the ground. The fields were checkerboard strips of golden wheat ready for harvest alternating with tilled strips of fallow ground. After about forty miles we took a gravel road eastward for about ten miles until we turned into the town of Regent.

I am not aware that we felt any great anticipation as we forged steadily toward our new home. We were a family unit and we lived and moved as such, accepting what the world gave us. I remember that Mother spent most of the time looking out the window with glum resignation. For myself, I was going off to college in a few weeks anyway.

Regent proved to be another dusty tank town along a branch railroad. We had always lived in towns like that, but to my mind Regent was the worst. The wide main street was unpaved, with enough room for people to park cars or wagons in the middle. The shabby business area consisted of about two blocks of low wooden buildings. The bank was a narrow frame building with an apartment in the back where we would live. There was a small back yard with a few wisps of struggling grass and a ramshackle garage. In its favor, Regent had a water tower and city water.

This part of North Dakota was still frontier country in many respects. The county seat, Mott, had a a population of about 1,200. Presumably there was a court house, although I don't recall it. There was a minimal J. C. Penny store, a movie theater, a bowling alley, a dance hall, and the usual array of small businesses related to agriculture. A distinctive feature was a large, wooden, wild-west hotel with a portico around it. This was the town where Uncle Maurice and his cowboy comrades had ridden down the main street whooping, hollering, and firing their pistols.

My most vivid memory of Regent is of the day we moved into our little apartment in the back of the bank. As Mom looked out of the window at that bleak environment, exiled from her friends and family, she wept inconsolably. She adjusted eventually: her view of all the vicissitudes of her life was that she never had a chance to be settled – she always had to "adjust". She took a kind of resigned pride in the fact that she had always "adjusted."

Dad was back in North Dakota, where his banking career had begun. In some respects he fared well in Regent. Harold Bowers, the owner of the bank, was a remarkable man whom Dad and Mom admired enormously. Bowers had become an officer of the Bank of North Dakota and was often in Bismarck. He was thankful to have a reliable, experienced small-town banker like Dad to run the bank when he was away. Dad was grateful that Bowers had saved him from the ignominy and desperation of unemployment. But Dad did not recover his former good spirits. As isolation and the disruption of war took over, he immersed himself in his work while family and social activities declined. The years of stress and disappointment had taken their toll.

Dad did not expect much from life, and he accepted what life gave him. Mom knew that life could be better, but she had to make do with what we had, and she did so without complaint. The dominant objective of Dad's life was to be a provider for his family, and he had a Depression-level concept of what providing was. Given his lack of education and opportunity, a roof over our heads, food on the table, and a car in the garage were the most he expected. In Regent Dad had reached his final destination. He had not made much progress across the bridge.

At this point I left the cocoon of my family. A few weeks after we moved to Regent, I went off to Concordia College for a year and then into the army for almost three years. The third generation was beginning its own journey across the bridge.

THE THIRD GENERATION:
THE CROSSING COMPLETED
(1942-1946)

Choosing a College

As the first of my family to go to college, I took a major step across the bridge that led to mainstream America. I was seventeen when I graduated from Alberta High School in May 1942, a year ahead of the usual graduation age. Skipping the second grade proved to be fortunate. I could take one year of college work before the draft called, and no one could predict what would happen after that. Despite the fact that Dad was losing his job at Alberta, it was settled that I would go to college, at least for a year. In my senior class of thirty-one, I was the only one who went directly on to college.

The natural place to go was Concordia College in Moorhead, Minnesota. Concordia was an institution of the Norwegian Lutheran Church. At that time the college was a struggling institution with approximately five hundred students. It lacked the long-established prestige of Luther College, Decorah, Iowa, or the financial resources of St. Olaf College, in Northfield, Minnesota, not far from the Twin Cities. But Concordia was the closest to Alberta and Regent, and that settled the matter.

I had only the vaguest notion of what I wanted to study. In addition to long-standing aspirations to the ministry, I had developed a strong interest in music and the violin, which I wished to pursue. When the Concordia catalog arrived, Mom and I sat at the dining room table, trying to puzzle out the bewildering array of departments, majors and minors, and courses. We had no idea what distribution requirements or credit hours were. Dad did not attempt to participate in this process. He probably would not have understood it, and he would have been embarrassed by not being able to fulfill the paternal role of decision maker. Furthermore, his job at the Alberta State Bank was in the process of disappearing, and he did not know how he would pay for college.

Some time in the late summer, before the move to Regent took place, Mom and Dad drove to Moorhead with me to visit Concordia. We were met by Dr. Peter A. Anderson, a perky, gray-haired man who was in charge of admissions and had many other administrative duties. I soon discovered that he was a wonderful, helpful man. His initials, as well as his concern for students, led him to be called "Pa" Anderson.

By the time I enrolled at Concordia the family was settled in Regent. Dad drove me to Moorhead, a distance of about 350 miles. When we arrived we were shown to my dormitory, an elderly building called South Hall. My room was next to the last at the end of the first floor corridor. The rooms were narrow, with two single beds, two rickety chests, and a place behind the door to hang clothes. Dad's eyes were wet when he left me. I know how he felt. I felt the same way when I took Julia and Tom to college. When they got settled in their rooms they were restless at having me around, and I could see that they were eager for me to be on my way. I suppose I was the same way until Dad left.

Photo – Earl Reitan as freshman,
Concordia College, 1942

For the first few days I did not have a room mate, since the draft was wreaking havoc with male students. A few days later, in walked a big, shy, good-looking, redheaded football player named Clarence Modine. He had enrolled late since he had been home finishing up the harvest. Our relationship demonstrated the maxim that opposites attract. I was the smart, articulate little guy with glasses. He was the big, slow-spoken football player. He gave me protection from hazing, and I contributed wit and brain power to the team. We got along remarkably well, and we continued as room mates after the war.

In the meantime I had made some good friends. In the next room were Ralph Livdahl and Jim Geerdes. They were both "presems" (preseminary students). Livdahl was quiet and studious and Geerdes was a lively extrovert. In another room was Norval Wigtil, another presem. Since every entry into the cafeteria was a crisis for shy, insecure freshmen, we four agreed to eat together, which would avoid having to sit with someone we did not know, or – even worse – eat alone.

The most impressive of the new freshmen in our corridor was Marcus Gravdal, son of a Lutheran minister, who was also a presem. Gravdal had an imposing appearance, a rich, resonant voice, and a degree of sophistication about the church and the college that the rest of us lacked. Gravdal's room became the center of late-evening seminars on the faculty and students, including assessments of the girls. With the catalog and last year's yearbook in hand, we went over the faculty, one by one, discussing their characteristics and qualifications, amplified by rumors and our own brief personal experiences. Some of the sophomores chipped in with the wisdom typical of that advanced level of higher education.

I learned, for example, that Dr. Skalet, who taught Latin and Greek, was highly respected as a scholar because he had a Ph.D. degree, which few Concordia faculty possessed in those days. His Ph.D. was from Johns Hopkins, a university that I had never heard of because it did not have a nationally recognized football team. I had never heard of Ph.D.s either. Probably at that time the seed was planted in my mind that I would like to be a Ph.D. and enjoy the respect given to Skalet.

At the end of my corridor was a room occupied by Nels Mugaas, an elderly Norwegian bachelor who was supervisor of buildings and grounds. Mugaas was a short, stocky man who had spent the better part of his life living in the dormitory with bumptious and noisy young males. He was always addressed by his first name. He used the same lavatory that we did, and in general there was a spirit of camaraderie and good-natured joshing between him and the students. It was known that on occasion he had advanced small loans to help students in financial difficulty. Rumor was that he kept his money in a box under his bed. Nels was comparatively patient with his living conditions, but at times the noise would become too much and he came out in the corridor and began shouting at us.

Classes

My classes met in the Old Main Building, a distinguished stone structure with columns in the front and an interior dominated by varnished woodwork. Instead of desks, as in high school, we sat in chairs with arms. It was to me a delightful surprise to find that in my classes I was referred to, not by my first name, as in high school, but as Mr. Reitan (pronounced Rye-tawn). I felt then, and still do, that this form of address made an important distinction between high school and college, because it established the adult nature of the latter. Throughout my own career as a university professor I always addressed students as Mr. or Miss, despite the move toward informality that came in the sixties.

I was determined to continue my interest in music, and I registered for Harmony I. My adviser sent me to meet with Paul J. Christiansen, son of the famous director of the St. Olaf Choir, F. Melius Christiansen. Paul J. had already made the Concordia Choir the rival of the St. Olaf Choir, then led by his brother, Olaf. Paul J. seemed dubious about me as a music major, probably because I had had so little formal training. He explained patiently that music was a field that required a great deal of talent and effort, and which was expensive in terms of lessons. He was a kindly man, and as such he wisely advised me to think of something else, but I was persistent and he let me follow my dream.

I quickly established myself as a student. Harmony I was taught by Sigvald Thompson, a superb musician without much opportunity at that time to exercise his talents. He began by showing that the overtones of a vibrating string provide the sounds on which chords and the notes of the scale are based. Since music students do not tend to be scientifically inclined, Thompson's venture into the physics of sound left many in the class confused, and when freshmen are confused they panic.

I understood well enough what Thompson was doing. That evening in the dorm I explained the lecture to another harmony student who lived in my corridor. He told a friend, who also came for tutoring. Soon half a dozen freshman harmony students were crowded into my little room while I explained Thompson's principles and the reason for them. The climax came about 10:00 PM when a trumpet player named Gordon Johnson, his unruly shock of hair flying, rushed into my room, harmony book in hand, and exclaimed desperately: "They say there's somebody here who understands this stuff!"

My college teaching career began my first day as a student, and I am happy that it did not end until my retirement.

My career as an historian was also foreshadowed in my first week. I was enrolled in European History I, taught by Miss Agnes Ellingsen, a tall, rangy, formidable woman who used the recitation method, asking questions in a hectoring manner until the students were scared stiff. The course began with background material on Medieval and Renaissance Europe, but it really got down to business with the Reformation. Until that time I had not been called upon and I had cowered in my seat, hoping she would not pick on me.

After two class periods Miss Ellingsen assigned the first half of the chapter on the Reformation. I found the chapter so interesting that I went on to the end. When we took up the chapter in class, the recitation went well enough at first. Then Miss Ellingsen asked a question to which no one had an answer. I raised my trembling hand and answered it in a quaking voice.

Miss Ellingsen asked another question. Again, silence. This time I answered the question more confidently. Miss Ellingsen looked pleased.

When the same thing happened a third time, she glared at the class and asked: "Why don't the rest of you know anything about this material?"

The students protested that the last several questions dealt with the second half of the chapter, which had not been assigned.

She turned to me. "Well, Mr. Reitan," she asked, "how do you happen to know so much about this?"

I answered, truthfully, that I had gotten interested and had read ahead to the end of the chapter. It will come as no surprise to learn that thereafter I was teacher's pet. I loved history and it came easily to me (the two usually go together, whatever the subject), and it is not surprising that history became my lifetime career.

Concordia College was conceived of as a Christian community, and, more specifically, as a Lutheran community. The Christian faith was everywhere present, from the college motto (*Sole Deo Gloria*) and the college hymn to everyday practices such as evening devotions in the dorms. Four semesters of religion were required. We did not study religion as an academic subject. The purpose of religion courses was to strengthen the Lutheran convictions that most students already possessed.

Daily chapel was an important part of Concordia's concept of a Christian college. The chapel was in the center of Old Main on the second floor. It seated about four hundred people on the main floor and had a balcony on three sides. Faculty and students alike were required to attend chapel, which convened five days a week. The faculty sat in the back row, most of them in the same seat every day. I saw the faculty daily and I soon got to know them, especially since we discussed them in Gravdal's late-evening seminars.

Even if one did not wish to go to chapel, there was little choice in the matter. The students were given assigned seats and attendance was checked. At chapel time there were no classes, the library and the cafeteria were closed, the dorms were deserted, and there was no place on campus to go without being conspicuous. Most of the speakers were local clergymen or from the religion faculty, but occasionally there was an outside speaker. Sometimes the Concordia College choir sang, which was always a treat.

Dr. Johnshoy, who taught philosophy and religion, spoke about once a month. His was an imposing presence, with a rich deep voice and a shock of bristling hair that outlined his face and brow like a Byzantine halo. Johnshoy was regarded as the most learned of the religion faculty. Most presems planned to major in philosophy, which at that time meant majoring in Johnshoy.

I was told with respect verging on awe that when he read the text in chapel he used a Greek New Testament from which he translated extemporaneously into elegant English. One time, however, he inadvertently left his New Testament open on the podium, and for some reason I saw it. I discovered that he had the Greek text on one page with the English text facing it. Although I saw no reason then (or now) to question his competence in New Testament Greek, this discovery took some of the mystery out of his reading of the text.

Life at Concordia College

My parents paid for my tuition, room, and board, but for spending money I had a job sweeping classrooms. When my parents and I met with "Pa" Anderson before I came to Concordia, arrangements were made for me to be employed by the college under a New Deal agency, the National Youth Administration (NYA), which provided money that colleges could use to help students earn part of their expenses. I worked from 3:00 to 5:00 PM sweeping classrooms and cleaning the johns in Old Main. My pay was ten cents per hour, or one dollar per week. Fortunately, having grown up in a thrifty family I was pretty much able to get by on whatever money I had. As a Republican small-town banker, Dad had opposed Roosevelt and the New Deal, but now I was a beneficiary of one of Roosevelt's programs.

Few Concordia students at that time had money to spend on clothes, apart from the necessities. However, there was a dress code based on a sense of propriety. I always wore a shirt and tie, pants, shined shoes, and a jacket or sweater. I did not have many clothes, and their style was "North Dakota Common." Almost all students dressed similarly but some, like Gravdal, who wore a suit, tie, and detachable starched collar, dressed better. The girls wore dresses or blouses and skirts, usually with saddle shoes and bobby sox. In a cold climate, sweaters were part of students' dress much of the academic year. Modern scruffiness simply did not exist.

On Sunday everyone got dressed up with a suit, white shirt, and tie (the girls in hose, heels, and their best dresses) and the students walked down the street to Trinity Lutheran Church for morning services. On sunny mornings in the autumn or spring the long line of nicely-dressed students walking to church, the girls' heels clicking on the sidewalks, was indeed a splendid sight.

At Concordia College Lutheran morality was required and was strictly enforced. Students who lived in town or in off-campus student housing were less subject to control, but if they broke the rules there was always the risk of discovery and expulsion. The door of the men's dorm was locked at 10:30 P.M. Anyone who was out beyond that time had to ring the bell and be admitted by the dorm director, who would want an explanation. Special arrangements were made for those few students whose jobs required them to stay out late. The girls were even more tightly restricted: they were required to sign out and sign in whenever they left the campus.

Drinking, swearing, dancing, and card-playing were strictly forbidden. There were always some students, male and female, who defied these restrictions, either because they wanted to do the forbidden things or they found excitement in defying authority. If they continued despite prayer and warnings, they would be expelled, although the college desperately needed every fee-paying student it could get. However, most Concordia students had powerful consciences and little money to waste on self-indulgence. In those days before the pill, sexual morality was reinforced by the threat of pregnancy.

Concordia's students came from a highly homogeneous population. They were overwhelmingly Lutheran, and most of them were Norwegian-American in origin. By and large, students from Minnesota seemed a little more polished than students from North Dakota (Fargo excepted). Students from Montana were a lively and self-aware bunch with a distinctive western openness and a strong *esprit de corps*. Students who came from larger towns had a little more social aplomb than those from tank towns like Alberta or Regent or off the farm.

A special group were the P.K.s (preachers' kids), of whom Concordia enrolled many. They had the advantage of growing up in a household where one or both parents had a college degree and education was important. On the other hand, life in the parsonage set the P.K. apart from his or her high school classmates. There was a belief that P.K.s, when liberated from the confining environment of the parsonage, would celebrate their freedom by running amuck. I am sure that some instances of that kind occurred. Most P.K.s, in my experience, were responsible, hard-working students. Many of the men studied for the ministry. In some cases, it might have been better for them if they had sought other careers, but the ministry was what they knew and felt comfortable with.

Students from Fargo and Moorhead, some of them P.K.s or the offspring of Concordia professors, had big advantages over the rest of us. They had attended large high schools with a variety of courses and extracurricular activities. They had grown up in an urban community. Compared to New York, Chicago, or Minneapolis, Fargo-Moorhead wasn't much. Compared to Alberta or Regent, Fargo-Moorhead was a metropolis.

Entertainment

Much of the entertainment at Concordia was provided by the college in the form of football and basketball games, plays, concerts, the Artists Series, and the like. Saturday night was the time for going to the movies to the extent that the students could afford it, which for me was not often. Visiting dance halls or taverns was sufficient cause for expulsion. Very few students had cars, so they walked or went by city bus. I had never before lived in a town that had a movie theater, which was one of my criteria of a real city. Fargo had several and Moorhead had one.

Since my room mate was a star football player, I enjoyed going to the games. I had never seen eleven-man football before; at first I was amazed at seeing twenty-two players milling around on the field at the same time. Basketball was a familiar sport, but in Concordia's little gym it was a rather congested affair. Concordia's coach, Jake Christiansen, was a brother of Paul J. He exhibited a rough exterior, but he had a heart of gold and was an outstanding football coach, making the most of average material. He was less successful in basketball, where his slow footed Norwegians were too easily outclassed.

A special opportunity to hear good music was the Artists Series, which Concordia sponsored in cooperation with neighboring Moorhead State Teachers College. The series consisted of four concerts per year. The price of admission was included in the student activity fee. In my freshman year I heard Nathan Milstein, the great violinist, and I recall vividly how thrilling it was. This was the first time that I heard a concert violinist in person, although I had heard violinists on the Sunday afternoon broadcasts of the New York Philharmonic. I was walking on air when I returned to the campus.

Sunday morning was occupied by religious activities, beginning at 8:30 with Mission Crusaders, a student group that met in the college chapel. Then the students walked down the street to Trinity Lutheran church for morning worship. Occasionally we visited some other Lutheran church. Clarence Modine was Swedish Lutheran, and some times I went with him to the Swedish church. After church we returned to campus for Sunday dinner in the cafeteria. Sunday afternoon was a good time to roam around and find something to do outdoors. Luther League, which was a religious program held in the chapel, met at 6:30 Sunday evening, and after that was study time.

Some Hazards Avoided

Concordia College had another Reitan (no relation to me) who was quite a campus character. He was a junior named Henry ("Red") Reitan. He engaged in a variety of student activities, including quarter-backing the football team. We became involved in an unusual way. The year before, "Red" Reitan had enjoyed a great success as a prankster. One of the students living in the dorm sang Norwegian songs, accompanying himself on the guitar. He would practice his art in the lounge, and the wretchedness of his singing and his comical Norwegian accent made him a laughing stock. When the Fargo Theater held an amateur contest, "Red" Reitan persuaded this gullible butt that he was a fine singer and should try his luck.

Organized by "Red" and a few confederates, the Concordia students packed the theater for the amateur contest, which would be decided by applause from the audience. As expected, the unwary victim of their flattery made a fool of himself, but he won the prize because the Concordia students clapped and shouted furiously when the audience was invited to pick the winner. "Red's" prank was still the talk of the campus when I arrived.

What does this anecdote have to do with me? Every afternoon I crossed the campus, violin under my arm, to the Conservatory building to practice. Someone got the idea that it would be fun to work the trick again. When the Fargo Theater announced another amateur contest, one of the conspirators listened to me practicing and discovered that my playing was more than bad enough to provide another evening of entertainment. One day, to my amazement, an upperclassman stopped me on campus and asked if I could play the *Meditation from Thais*. Soon I was surprised to find students whom I did not know asking about my violin playing, which left me puzzled, although naturally I welcomed the attention.

When he heard what was intended, "Red" Reitan put a stop to it. He told me that he wasn't going to have anyone named Reitan made a fool of on the stage of the Fargo Theater. As a result of that episode I began leaving my violin in my practice room on top of the piano, instead of carrying it conspicuously across campus. In my three full years at Concordia it was never stolen or tampered with, which perhaps says something about how different things were in those days. Or maybe it says something about Concordia students.

I came to the attention of the campus in another way that first semester. There was an intense rivalry between Concordia and Moorhead State Teachers College, just a few blocks away. For the previous several years, young males from each campus had attempted to destroy the Homecoming decorations of the other. One year, for example, Concordia students had written "Cobbers" (the college nickname) in gasoline on the MSTC football field and set the gasoline afire. MSTC students had retaliated.

As a result, the practice had developed that for three nights before Homecoming it was the duty of the male freshmen to guard the campus, staying up all night in shifts. Officious upperclassmen organized the shifts. Since October evenings in Moorhead were cool, the freshmen collected dead tree branches and built a bonfire in the street to keep warm. Somehow this practice was tolerated by the college and the Moorhead fire department, but the escapade in which I was involved in my freshman year brought it to an end.

The night before Homecoming, about midnight, as we freshmen were standing around passing the hours with idle chatter, we saw a suspicious character sneaking through the trees and bushes near Fjelstad Hall, a girls dormitory. Immediately the hue and cry went up and we took off after him. Finding himself discovered, the young man quick-wittedly pointed to the roof of

Fjelstad Hall, where a stream of silvery smoke was etched in the night sky by a full moon.

"Fjelstad Hall is on fire," he shouted, as he hurried away. "Fjelstad Hall is on fire," the excited freshmen cried, losing sight of their quarry in the process.

Someone called the fire department, and in no time at all firemen, engines roaring, lights blazing, came rushing to the campus. "Pa" Anderson, dressed in pajamas and bathrobe, appeared on the scene, disheveled gray hair flying in the cold night air. The girls came rushing out of the dorm, wearing whatever they could put on.

Cooler heads immediately saw that the smoke was rising from a flue. "Pa" Anderson apologized to the firemen, who replied that they were glad it was not a real fire. "Pa" told us to go back to our rooms, which we were glad to do, because we were tired and cold, to say nothing of being embarrassed.

Now my own personal experience of notoriety. The first night, about 11:00 P.M., two young men in a new car came racing through the campus, swerving at groups of freshmen standing along the street. They disappeared for a while, and then we heard the roar of their engine as they accelerated to come back. This time they swerved near our fire and sent sparks flying from the ashes.

When they came the third time I took a tree limb from our fuel supply, rushed into the street, and struck a blow which left a big dent in the right front fender of the car. The car raced away as the freshmen cheered and patted me on the back. I was the hero of the hour.

The occupants of the car turned out to be Concordia sophomores, one of them the son of a local minister, whose new car they were driving. The next day they caught me in an isolated location on campus, shoved me up against a wall, and said they would beat me up if I didn't pay for the cost of repair.

Of course I didn't have the money, but on my side I had Clarence Modine and the football team. Some of them crowded into the room which Cal and I shared and told me not to worry about those guys. Even Ray Grande, our star halfback and a tough hombre, was there. The sophomores who had driven the car were informed in no uncertain terms that they got what they deserved and to lay off me. Needless to say, I heard nothing more about paying for the damage. To my knowledge, the administration knew nothing about the incident. If they did, they were smart enough to let the students settle their own problems.

My freshman year at Concordia College was another turning point in my life. Concordia became a new and larger family. Concordia was large enough to offer many new challenges, but college was small enough for each student to feel known and find a body of friends. The faculty and students were my kind of people, yet varied enough to widen my horizons enormously. At Concordia I made good progress across the bridge that led from my immigrant grandparents through my parents to a larger world, and with good companions to share the experience and assist me on my way.

"You're in the Army Now"

On May 3, 1943 I turned eighteen. I registered for the draft in Regent, and shortly thereafter I received my notice from the Hettinger County Draft Board with the familiar salutation: "Greetings." As a town dweller in a rural county, they took me as soon as possible. I received orders to report to Ft. Snelling, Minnesota for induction in September. The draftees reported at the Mott railroad station about 3:00 A.M. on a cold night. Dad and I waited uneasily for the train; there were a few murmurs among the draftees and their families, but most people stood silently. The train pulled into the station. Dad kissed me. He had not done that for a long time. The draftees got on the train, and the brakeman waved his lantern. Dad stood on the platform, watching, as the train pulled out of the station into the darkness.

When I was inducted into the U. S. Army, my life was no longer closely linked with my family or the Norwegian-American community. Most draftees left behind a life that was largely local, whether it was the urban neighborhood, the small town, or the farm. We were swept into a huge institution that put its members in intimate contact with men drawn from all parts of the country. My own background had been especially restricted, and I became a fascinated observer of the kaleidoscope of people, places, and experiences that the U. S. Army offered.

I liked the orderly routines of the army. Discipline was no problem: I was accustomed to accepting the commands of authorities. I had always tried to do the right thing, and the army left no doubt as to what that was. I did not swear, drink, smoke, gamble, or run around with loose women. I did not even use bad grammar. I was always properly dressed, gave snappy salutes, picked up the special terminology of the army quickly, and enjoyed the Saturday morning parade. I was never in trouble, nor did I trouble anyone else. I kept a low profile, and no one paid much attention to me as I was swept along on the tide of global war.

I did my seventeen-week basic training at Camp Roberts, California. On the trip I slept in a Pullman berth, ate in the dining car, and had my first view of mountains. The training was physically strenuous, especially for someone like myself, who was small and immature, but I held up reasonably well. The camp was in a beautiful semidesert area, and the winter weather was crisp and cool and pleasantly warm in the afternoon. We did a lot of marching with a heavy rifle and pack, plus firing a variety of infantry weapons. We attended lectures on military courtesy, discipline, hygiene, and the like. The food was good and abundant, and we had a new movie twice a week. I had good legs and feet and could shoot a rifle, and that was mainly what was required.

I had another talent. The first day Sergeant Chandler, a southern hillbilly noncom, identified me as a northern college boy and put me on latrine detail. With the experience I had gained at home and at Concordia, cleaning the stools was a job that I could handle. The other members of the detail joined in with such rookie enthusiasm that our latrine got the highest possible rating. Sergeant Chandler knew a winner when he saw one. With typical army logic, he rewarded us for our good work by keeping us on latrine detail for the remaining sixteen weeks.

Photo – Earl Reitan & comrade,
Camp Roberts, CA 1943

At Camp Roberts I continued my wide-ranging reading. One evening, lacking something better to do, I picked up a copy of The *Infantry Journal*, which had an article on protection from tropical diseases. The next day, as luck would have it, Captain Green, the company commander, was scheduled to teach a class on hygiene. When he brought up tropical diseases, I had a repeat of my success with Miss Ellingsen.

After I had responded to several questions, Captain Green asked me if I was a premedical student. I replied, truthfully, that I had read an article in *The Infantry Journal*. That did it! He called upon me to come to the front and take over the class, and placed a commendation on my record. Afterwards, Sergeant Chandler congratulated me. But he did not take me off latrine detail.

In February 1944, I emerged from Camp Roberts as a rifleman. The little wooden rifle that Dad had made for me in Grove City, the Daisy air rifle in Bay City, and the 20-gauge shotgun in Alberta, had morphed into a powerful, accurate, 9 1/2 pound Garand M-1 rifle and a sharpshooter medal. The infantry was the least popular part of the army, and with good reason. I had hoped that my year of college would bring acceptance into the Army Special Training Program (ASTP) where I wanted to learn a foreign language and be a translator. By the time I left Camp

Roberts, the army had become aware of a great attrition of riflemen. ASTP was being shut down and the soldiers enrolled in the program were being sent to the infantry anyway. So my fate was settled.

Photo – Family Portrait, February, 1944

I was given orders to report to Ft. Meade, Maryland (near Baltimore) after a furlough. On the way I stopped at Regent for a few days, where my parents and siblings wanted to hear about the army and see my uniform. That lasted for about forty-five minutes, and then they returned to their usual activities. We went to Dickinson for a family portrait, the only one we ever had.

The trip to California had given me my first view of the mountains. The voyage overseas introduced me to the ocean (we did not get along very well), the Rock of Gibraltar, and Mount Vesuvius. We landed at Naples, my first glimpse of foreign soil. I was assigned as a rifleman to Company F, 7th Infantry Regiment, the Third Infantry Division. They were on the Anzio beach head, where I got my baptism of fire (and almost my quietus) on the drive to Rome. We attacked the morning after I arrived, and in the first hour we were hit by an artillery barrage that left five members of my platoon dead and fifteen wounded. It was a harrowing introduction to an experience that would be repeated many times.

After five days of combat I found myself marching with my victorious comrades down the main drag of Rome, past the Colosseum and the Forum, where so many victorious armies had passed before. Then my squad was posted to guard the Palazzo Venezia, where Mussolini had harangued the populace. It had been a memorable week for a young Minnesota-Norwegian who had turned nineteen just a month earlier.

Photo – Earl Reitan, Italy, 1944

The fall of Rome on June 5, 1944 was overshadowed by the D-Day landings in Normandy the next day. Then we returned to Naples to prepare for the landing in southern France. The weather was warm and sunny and the land was beautiful, but the people were desperate. Children lined up with buckets to take the leftovers from our mess kits, and I usually managed to save something for them. One of the children, I learned many years later, grew up to be the movie star, Sophia Loren.

In early August we were ready to leave. By that time, Patton's Third Army was racing across France and other Allied forces were driving into Belgium and approaching the German border. As we waited in the troopships in Naples harbor, Winston Churchill came by in a PT boat, giving his V-for-Victory salute. I still recall his flying white locks of hair and his red face, but the famous cigar was missing.

"The Second D-Day" took place on August 15, 1944. Company F was in the first wave. In the early morning darkness, heavily laden with rifles, ammunition, and supplies, we climbed down the rope net into our bobbing little landing craft. As we started toward shore, a fierce naval barrage arose from shadowy warships, their muzzle blasts piercing the gloom. Then the sky turned pink and the contours of the Riviera became visible. Overhead came vast fleets of bombers; out of a cloud of dust arose a mighty roar, as they dropped their bombs on the landing sites. Suddenly the sky was filled with paratroops, fluttering down to meet us.

As we neared the shore, the boat next to us hit a mine and blew up, scattering debris into our boat. Nineteen men from Company F were lost. When our boat scraped on the sand, the front went down and we splashed through the water onto a deserted beach. My platoon sergeant, Sergeant Earl Swanson of Minneapolis, ordered me to fire a rifle grenade at a house at the edge of the beach. My grenade hit its target, but the house was deserted. Then we moved inland, marching through the night toward Marseilles.

The next morning I was wounded in the knee by a German mortar shell. I was taken from the beach to a hospital ship, and from there to an army hospital in Naples, where I spent almost three months. In the fall of 1944 the shortage of riflemen had become acute. Although a wound in the knee was usually an exit ticket from the infantry, I was sent to a camp near Rome for additional conditioning before returning to my unit.

Facing a return to combat, I wrote a letter home that expressed my feelings at the time. Mother said she kept it on her dresser, and every time she read it her eyes filled with tears.

Somewhere in Italy

October 4, 1944

Dear folks,

I don't have anything to say tonight but I thought I would write anyway; it's almost as good as a conversation.

Do you ever wonder what I look like as a soldier? Well, right now I am sitting on one of the six canvas folding cots ranged around the side of our tent, and an apple box is my writing table. I am all alone tonight as the other fellows are all on guard. A short stub of a candle furnishes the only light and throws weird shadows into the semi-dark corners of the tent. The big black tent seems very strong and reassuring and the little candle makes everything in its small orbit seem very friendly. . . . At the present, home seems like heaven; something very distant that you aren't counting on for a long time – if ever.

Now, if we will step over to the flap which is the door, we will see a very beautiful sight. Our tent is on the second of a series of terraces on the side of a hill which is the U end of a large natural amphitheater. In the center of this bowl is a clear lake, almost artificial looking. The full moon has just risen above the cut at the other end and the lake is covered with a sparking silver sheen, while a few dark puffs of cloud display the edge of the lining people are always putting so much hope in. The pointed tents which surround the lake are all bathed in pale moonlight. In a few minutes we will hear the bugle sounding Taps. The notes echoing through the hills add an ethereal harmony which sounds somewhat like a person singing into the strings of a piano.

Now the eyelids are getting heavy and another day is coming – first call at six thirty. Up and at 'em! So for now it's Good night.

Love,
Earl

Early in November, as the skies were becoming gray and cold, I was loaded with other returning GIs on a troopship bound for Marseilles. Our mood was somber. There was none of the excitement we had felt in Naples harbor when we had left for the Riviera landing, cheered on by none other than Winston Churchill himself. I returned to F Company, where I served as a rifleman through the brutal winter of 1944-45. Our campaign in "the Colmar Pocket" was completed in February 1945, and my outfit was restocked with fresh riflemen from the States. The wound in my knee was still not fully healed, and I became a mail clerk at a replacement depot in France.

In the meantime, my intellectual horizons were expanding. While recovering in Naples from my wound, I had attended the opera, visited the remains of Pompeii, and taken other tours in the area. While stationed in France I made several trips to Paris, where the Metro, the Louvre, and other tourist attractions were free to GIs. I recall roaming through a nearly-deserted Louvre, when I turned a corner and there – under a spotlight – was the Venus de Milo. It stopped me in my tracks. I went on a bus tour to the Pyrenees and Lourdes ("The Song of Bernadette" was an Academy Award winner in 1943), and met my Concordia classmate, Jim Geerdes, in Rheims.

As company mail clerk at the replacement depot, I was responsible for dissemination of the many paperback books that American publishers had made available, free of charge, for the troops overseas. With first choice of the books, I read everything from English translations of Greek and Roman classics to famous novels by Dickens and Dostoevsky to mysteries by Agatha Christie and Ellery Queen. I kept up with world affairs through *Stars and Stripes* and *Yank*, and heard popular music on Armed Forces Radio. I saw innumerable wartime movies and developed a crush on Jeanne Crain.

When the war in Europe ended, we were busy processing unhappy GIs for transfer to the Pacific theater. Suddenly the news came that an atom bomb had been dropped on Japan, and another bomb three days later. The Emperor called for surrender. The war was over! I am well aware of the dangers to the world of nuclear weapons, but I cannot find it in my mind or heart to condemn the use of them to prevent the invasion of Japan.

Before returning home, this young Norwegian-American enjoyed an unusual experience. The British government, as a modest repayment of American Lend-Lease aid, offered to enroll two hundred American soldiers as students in British universities. I applied and was accepted. From October through Christmas, 1945, I was a student at the University of Glasgow, in Scotland. I lived with six other GIs at No. 7, Hillhead Street, near the campus. I attended lectures in Moral Philosophy and Shakespeare, and took trips to Edinburgh, the Highlands, and the border country. I had a Scottish girlfriend (a student at the university), and we went out together with others in my house and their girlfriends. As a sign of my emancipation, I learned to dance and was quite graceful, even while wearing my heavy army boots.

I had one more close call before I made it home. I was among several hundred GIs stuffed into a small British aircraft carrier that left Plymouth for New York in early January 1946. We ran into heavy storms and I was terribly seasick. My appendix ruptured and emergency surgery at sea was necessary. Acute peritonitis set in, which had been ninety-five percent fatal in the past. The new wonder drug, penicillin, saved my life. An ambulance was waiting at the dock in New York City to take me to Halloran Hospital. While I was in this helpless condition, one of my fellow Americans, whom I had risked my life to protect, stole my barracks bag with my uniform and souvenirs.

When I awoke the next morning, the sun was shining in the windows, the radio was playing big band music, and someone offered me the New York *Daily News*. I was in a bed behind a screen where (I learned later) they put patients who were expected to die. That morning a parade of doctors came to see this kid who was still alive after such an ordeal. I was home – sort of.

My recovery took three months. Dad wanted to come to New York City to see me, but I persuaded him to wait until I was more fully recovered. In May I went home on furlough, a mere shadow of myself. As the train raced along the Burlington line from Chicago to the Twin Cities, I glanced idly out the window to view Lake Pepin. There it was: Point-no-Point! Before I could sit up to look, the train had flashed through Bay City. I wanted to see more, but Bay City vanished as quickly as it had appeared.

Memories flooded my mind and swelled my heart: a red-haired, freckle-faced boy in bib overalls, the little bungalow overlooking the mighty Mississippi, the butternut tree, Feldman, Adolph Anderson, Jimmy Reed, Terry, Miss Lien, and the awesome story of the sorcerer's apprentice. "Time is – Time was – Time never more shall be." The glowing head had spoken truth.

There was nothing triumphant about my homecoming: no parade, no shower of ticker tape, no flags flying and bands playing, no girls in the street waiting to be kissed. I had lost my insignia, medals, and combat infantry badge when my barracks bag was stolen. In my unadorned, ill-fitting uniform, I looked like a fresh recruit. I had no souvenirs to show or gifts to give. I had come back to a town where I knew no one. No matter. I was home.

Back to Concordia

After spending some time recuperating in Regent, I reported to Mayo Army General Hospital at Galesburg, Illinois, for the removal of my appendix, which completed my medical treatment. I was honorably discharged from the U. S. Army at Ft. Sheridan, Illinois, in June 1946. I celebrated by going to the magnificent Chicago Theater to hear Frank Sinatra.

For our first family vacation since moving to Regent, Dad rented a cottage for a week at Lake Koronis, not far from Grove City. The cottage provided an opportunity to get reacquainted with my parents and siblings, and a long-delayed opportunity to visit the Reitan and Jensen relatives. But I had other things on my mind.

In the hospital I had read John P. Marquand's popular novel, "H. M. Pulham, Esq" (1941). Marquand wrote novels about proper Bostonians. Pulham, the main character, had grown up in a brownstone mansion on Beacon Hill prior to World War I. He had gone to the right schools, met the right friends, joined the right clubs, and been tagged by one and all to marry the right girl from an equally right family. Before the wedding could take place, he had been called away by the war.

When Pulham returned from military service overseas, he stopped briefly in New York City to visit a friend, who offered him a job on a newspaper in that most exciting of cities. At the same time he met a delightful, emancipated young woman with whom he had an all-too-brief fling. But filial duty called him back to Boston where his family, friends, and fiancee were awaiting him. Somehow, for one reason or another, none of which was very compelling, he did not make it back to New York. He remained in Boston, where he lived out the stable, boring existence into which he had been born.

This novel framed the great question: "Should I break with the bonds of my past and make a fresh start?" I was twenty-one years old, with my adult life in front of me. I had seen something of the world and had an idea of its possibilities. With the support of the GI Bill, I could go any place in the country to complete my college education. I thought of going east to Harvard or Columbia, or west to some California university. I sent for a catalog from the

University of Denver. In the U.S. Army no one could ever pronounce my name, and I considered changing it to Eric Alan Rydan.

Suddenly I realized that summer session was beginning at Concordia College. In the middle of the week I hopped a bus to Moorhead. Many familiar faces greeted me: "Pa" Anderson, Agnes Ellingsen, Sigvald Thompson, Geerdes, Livdahl, Gravdal, and Wigtil. Clarence Modine was there, and we became roommates again. It was wonderful! Concordia had become my new home and family. I stayed right there.

But a great change had taken place. I had crossed the bridge and was now on other side.

EPILOGUE:
ON THE OTHER SIDE OF THE BRIDGE
(1946-1994)

About Me

When I returned to Concordia College in June 1946, the faculty and the buildings seemed about the same, only a little older. The return of the GIs, however, changed the college dramatically. Enrollment rose to 1,100 students. The GIs were more mature than typical students, and strongly motivated. Faculty said the GIs were the best students they had ever had. The commitment of the college to the concept of a Christian community continued, but the reality changed. Veterans would not put up with the narrow, rigid rules and practices of the pre-war Concordia. Attendance at chapel was still required, but with enrollment nearly doubled, it became necessary to schedule two sessions. Since half the students were free at any one time, the library was open, the cafeteria was open for morning coffee, and no one became conspicuous by not attending chapel. Like many others, eventually I stopped going.

Photo – Earl Reitan at Concordia College, 1948

As a freshman, I had been overwhelmed by college life. The two years after the war were my true college days. With the GI bill, for the first time I had some money in my pockets. I knew that I no longer felt a call to the Lutheran ministry; I had crossed the bridge. I decided that I wanted to become a college professor. I majored in history, although I also completed my music major and continued with violin lessons. I participated in plays, wrote skits, and became something of a comedian. In August 1948, I graduated and prepared to go to graduate school.

One of my Concordia classmates, for reasons of his own, wanted to do graduate study at the University of Illinois. Without giving it much thought, I decided to go off to Illinois with him. I remember informing my parents of this decision. The back room of the bank had a large wall map of the United States; as we looked at it, Champaign-Urbana, Illinois seemed a long way away, and it was. The University of Illinois was a sharp break with my past. Concordia College was very much a part of the Norwegian-American community that I had grown up in. At the University of Illinois, I became part of a cosmopolitan student body, studying English and European history under distinguished professors.

In 1951-52 I had a one-year appointment at Pacific Lutheran College (now University) in Tacoma, Washington. When I left Concordia for Illinois, I had intended to teach at one of the Lutheran colleges, possibly Concordia itself. My year at Pacific Lutheran changed that. I discovered that my experience at a big state university had given me a new set of aspirations. I was ready for another step into mainstream America.

My Ph.D. degree was conferred in August 1954. I was offered a position in history at Illinois State University (then Illinois State Normal University), only fifty miles away. At the first meeting of the new faculty, I met the new director of a women's dorm. We were married two years later, and we have lived in Normal, Illinois ever since. I retired in September 1990.

About my Family

My last personal conversation with Dad took place when I was discharged from the Army. I told him that I did not intend to go into the ministry. I had decided to become a professor, and the GI

Bill made it possible for me to pursue my goal. I could tell that Dad was disappointed. He respected ministers and the church, and he knew nothing about colleges and professors.

The move to Regent had finally broken Dad's links with Grove City. During his last visit to Grove City, it was evident that Dad's energy was ebbing. Aunt Rose remarked to me how much he had declined. Many of his friends of yesteryear were gone; to others he was a dimly remembered relic of bygone days. They were uninterested in talking about the past, which was all that they and Dad had in common. Finally his Grove City roots had withered. Earnest Reitan had become a stranger in his old hometown.

Regent also weakened Dad's links with the Norwegian-American community. He had never shown much interest in his Norwegian background, nor did he speak Norwegian. His marriage to a Dane further reduced the influence of the Norwegian heritage in our family. Regent had a Lutheran church, but it was not the Evangelical (Norwegian) Lutheran Church. The population of the area was mixed and not dominated by Scandinavians, as in Meeker County.

Photo – Regent, ND
1945

Photo – Regent, ND
1949

Photo – Mom, 1968

Dad died in January 1950 at age 57, worn out by work, worry, and a pack of Chesterfields a day. It was a raw January day in Minnesota when Dad's body returned to Grove City for the last time. The funeral was held in the Norwegian Lutheran Church, and he was buried with his Reitan ancestors in the Reitan plot. At last he had returned to the roots that he had lost so long ago.

The night of the funeral, I slept on the sofa in Aunt Rose's parlor. In the middle of the night I heard Dad calling me: "Earl, Earl." I raised my head from my pillow and saw his face, bathed in golden light, across the room above the front door.

Again the voice called, "Earl, Earl." I sat up and tried to respond. Before I could reply, the vision faded and the voice was no more. I was shaken to the core. I knew that what I had seen was not an ordinary dream. Whatever the vision was, Dad was gone.

When Dad died, Mother decided to move to Moorhead. She found a job in the Concordia cafeteria and got her own apartment. In Moorhead, she achieved a degree of independence and confidence that would have surprised her in the days of her marriage. Involuntarily and unexpectedly, she earned that which young women today expect: her own career, income, apartment, and friends.

Mom gained a reputation as a baker, and was employed in that capacity in several places. She enjoyed the facilities of a larger city: Trinity Lutheran Church – a large congregation with a variety of activities, special events at Concordia College, a good public library, a modest but well-appointed arts center, the shopping facilities of Fargo and Moorhead, and a group of single women (mainly widows) with whom to associate. She never attempted to drive a car, but at last she had her own telephone. Fargo and Moorhead were among the most Norwegian cities outside of Norway, and she was still part of the Norwegian-American community. But she had moved farther across the bridge than she had ever expected.

Like me, my brothers and sister completed the journey across the bridge and reached the other side. During the war, Clayton had served in the navy, and he continued his education after the war. He received a Ph.D. degree from the University of Wisconsin in meteorology, and is now retired from Northern Illinois University, DeKalb. In 1947-48, my senior year, Phil enrolled as a freshman at Concordia. When he graduated from Concordia, Phil went to the University of Wisconsin where he took his Ph.D. degree in biology. He is now retired from Luther College, Decorah, Iowa. Norma graduated from Concordia and earned a degree in library science from Oklahoma State University. For many years she has been employed in a responsible position at the Library of Congress.

Looking Back

Why did the children of Earnest and Helene Reitan, neither of whom graduated from high school, all pursue learned professions? This memoir has probably answered that question already. We sprang from strong and determined grandparents and parents, and we grew up in a Norwegian-American culture that emphasized personal responsibility and hard work. We were baptized into a teaching church with a learned clergy and a deeply-rooted theology. The public schools and Concordia College played an important role. Mother was unquestionably the main influence: she was the civilizing force in our lives.

Ours has been, in many respects, a fortunate generation. We have been able to ride the wave of America's postwar greatness and prosperity, while Dad and Mom had to struggle through difficult times. Dad never saw his children settled in life, nor did he enjoy a comfortable retirement. I am glad that Mother lived to see better days.

Over the years, Grove City continued to draw me back; it was my equivalent of "the Old Country." On my trips from Illinois to Moorhead to visit Mother, I would occasionally go by way of Grove City to view again the family symbols: the church, the clock, and the graves. A few miles along the highway was "Auntwater," where I would see Aunt Rose and Uncle Ben. Sometimes I would see Aunt Lou and Aunt Beattie and Uncle Maurice too. Usually I would go out to the Jensen farm to see Uncle Christ and Aunt Vera, or take a few minutes to see Aunt Mary in Litchfield. When it became necessary for Mother to enter a nursing home, she returned to Litchfield and Meeker County, where her life had begun.

At Mother's funeral in October 1994 I noticed how shabby Grove City had become. The building that had once housed the Merchants and Farmers State Bank and "Central" stood vacant. Our former house badly needed a coat of paint. The Norwegian and Swedish Lutheran congregations had been amalgamated, and the funeral was held in the former Swedish church. The century-old Norwegian church had been sold and its lovely fittings dismantled. My cousin June (born the same day I was) had the clock.

Only the graveyard remained the same. I decided that I did not want to go back to Grove City again, except to join "Father" and "Mother," and Dad and Mom, in their eternal sleep.

ABOUT THE AUTHOR

Earl A. Reitan was born in Grove City, Mn in 1925. He received his B.A. degree from Concordia College, Moorhead, Mn (1948) and his Ph.D. degree in history from the University of Illinois (1954). Since 1954 he has been Professor of History (now emeritus) at Illinois State University, Normal, IL.

The Author

His academic specialty is eighteenth-century Britain. His first book was "George III: Tyrant or Constitutional Monarch?" (Boston: D. C. Heath, 1965). He is the author of "Politics, War, and Empire: The Rise of Britain to a World Power, 1688-1792" (Arlington Heights, IL: Harlan Davidson, 1994). He is co-author of "English Heritage" (3rd ed., Arlington Heights, IL: Harlan Davidson, 1999), a textbook on English History, for which he wrote the chapters on nineteenth and twentieth century Britain. His book entitled "Tory Radicalism: Margaret Thatcher, John Major, and the Transformation of Modern Britain, 1979-97" (Lanham, MD: Rowman & Littlefield) was published in 1997.

He is a veteran of World War II, having served as a rifleman with the Third Infantry Division on the Anzio beachhead, in the landing in southern France (where he was wounded), and in the Vosges and Colmar Pocket campaigns. He has published articles on battles in which his battalion was engaged.

His wife, Carol, is an executive with the Institute for Collaborative Solutions located in Bloomington, IL. They have two children: Julia, who lives in San Francisco, CA, and Thomas, Chagrin Falls, OH. They have two grandchildren, William Andrew and Mary Veronica of Chagrin Falls.

Sources and Acknowledgements

This book is based primarily upon personal memories of my family and myself as I was growing up. These memories may have been flawed when they were laid down, but they have not changed over the years. Basic facts about my grandfather and grandmother are based on their obituaries, amplified by stories told me by my father and mother. Special thanks are due to my cousin, Mrs. Donna Gilman, who provided me with copies of letters written by my grandfather, plus her personal recollections of my grandparents. I am indebted to Mrs. Joanne Foley for information about Alberta. The Stevens County Historical Society provided valuable newspaper articles about the Alberta school. My brothers, Clayton and Phil, have contributed memories of our family life.

Apparently I have always had the instincts of an historian. When I was a child I enjoyed hearing Dad talk about his early years. Later, when I was an established historian, I took advantage of several long car trips to question Mom about her family and our life in Grove City. Her memory was acute, and she provided much information relative to the first and second chapters. She maintained photograph albums for myself and my brothers, and these were the source of most of the photographs.

I wish to express gratitude for their assistance to my colleagues at Illinois State University, Mark Wyman and Ralph Bellas, and to my Concordia College classmates, Arland Fiske and Harland Nelson. Special thanks are due to Corinne Nelson for bringing to the manuscript the keen eye and sharp pencil of a professional editor.

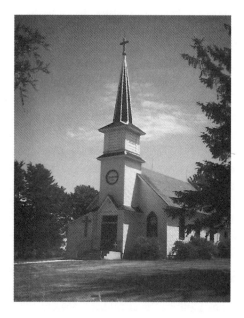

Photo – Tabor Church, rural Bay City.
Taken in 1980s

INDEX

A

Aamodt, Miss, 94
Acton, 36
Alaska, 15, 16
Alberta State Bank, 68, 69, 97, 98, 103
Anderson, Adolph, 44, 123
Anderson, Dr. Peter A., 104
appendix ruptured, 123
Arndahl, 27, 32
Atwater, 18, 22, 32, 62, 99
Auntwater. *See* Atwater

B

Bank of North Dakota, 101
Barnes' Bluff, 50
Bay City State Bank, 43
Bay City, WI, 42
Beardsley, Miss, 82
Bellas, Ralph, 135
bootleggers, 43, 44
Bowers, Harold, 101
Braun's gas station, 65
Bull, Ole - the Norwegian violinist, 57
Burlington Railroad, 46
butternut tree, 48, 123

C

Camp Roberts, California, 116
Campbell, Johnny - Players, 91
Champaign-Urbana, Illinois, 128
Chandler, Sgt., 116
chivaree, 44
Chokio, Mn., 81
Christiansen, F. Melius, 106
Christiansen, Jake, 111
Christiansen, Paul J., 106
Christmas, 45, 55, 58, 75, 84, 122
Concordia Choir, 106
Concordia College, 5, 98, 102, 103, 115, 127, 128, 131, 133, 135
Cutts, Mrs. Dr., 30

D

E

F

G

H

I

J

Jensen (Reitan), Caren Helene, 27
Jensen, aunts and uncles, 28
Jensen, Grandma - maternal grandmother, 27
Jensen, Jorgen, maternal grandfather, 27
Jensen, Uncle Christ, 27
Johnshoy, Dr., 108
Johnson, Gordon, 107

K

Kerlan, Mr. J. H., 78
Kindseth, Karen, 7
Kring, Albert and Minnie, 28

L

LaCrosse, 46
Lake Koronis, 124
Lake Minnewaska, 86
Lake Pepin, 42, 47, 50, 63, 123
Lake Superior, 14
Larson's Store, 66
Lewis, Sinclair, 89
Liedholm, Aaron, 26
Lien, Miss Laura, 52
Litchfield, 7, 8, 30, 36, 68, 132
Livdahl, Ralph, 105
Ludwig's Saloon, 67
lutefisk, 75
Luther College, 103, 131
Lutheran Normal School, 18

M

Mankato, 24, 78
Mayo Army General Hospital, 124
Meeker County, 7, 26, 129, 132
Merchants and Farmers State Bank, 26, 35, 39, 41, 62, 132
Milstein, Nathan, 111
Minneapolis, 7, 46
Minot, ND, 25
Mississippi River, 42
Mississippi salmon, 43
Model T Ford, 25, 40
Modine, Clarence, 104, 114
Moorhead State Teachers College, 111

Morris, Mn., 67
Mott, ND, 101
Mugaas, Nels, 105

N

National Youth Administration, 109
Nelson, Corinne, 135
Nelson, Harland, 135
Nelson, Roger, 20
Nelson, Uncle Maurice, 17
New Deal, 94
New London, 21
New World, 3
Northfield, 7, 103
Northwestern Elevator Company, 8
Norwegian Lutheran, 8, 9, 10, 11, 24, 32, 35, 39, 63, 70, 83, 84, 103, 130

O

Obrecht, Christy, 91
Old Country, 3, 35, 132
Olsen, Rev. C. Arthur, 84
Olson, Gov. Floyd B., 94
Orpha (Mrs. Adolph Anderson), 44, 61
Oslo, 5

P

P.K.s (preachers' kids), 110
Pacific Lutheran College, 128
Paulson, Miss, 79
pheasant, 25, 46, 75, 85, 86
Photo – Alberta State Bank, 66
Photo – Alberta, Mn – Our house, 70
Photo – Alberta, Mn – Trinity Lutheran Church. Taken in 1980s, 84
Photo – Alberta, Mn Consolidated School c. 1941, 77
Photo – Bay City – Earl, Clayton, Phil & Terry, 51
Photo – Bay City bungalow with Lake Pepin in background, 47
Photo – Bay City School, 52
Photo – Bay City State Bank, 43
Photo - C.C. Reitan Family, 4
Photo – Christian Clement Reitan, Karen Kindseth Reitan, 8
Photo – Dad, Mom, Aunt Evelyn, Uncle Carl, 16
Photo - Earl A. Reitan, 133
Photo – Earl Reitan & comrade, Camp Roberts, CA 1943, 117
Photo – Earl Reitan as freshman, Concordia College, 1942, 104
Photo – Earl Reitan at Concordia College, 1948, 127

Photo – Earl Reitan, Italy, 1944, 119
Photo – Family Portrait, February, 1944, 118
Photo – Grandma Albertina Jensen, 8
Photo – Grove City: Merchants & Farmers State Bank, 26; our house, 26
Photo – Grove City, Immanuel Lutheran Church, 12
Photo – Grove City, Reitan Gravestone, 12
Photo – Hastings, Mn. Spiral Bridge *c.* 1915, 62
Photo – Jensen Girls – Front, Caren Helene, Hilda Back, Mary, Minne, 9
Photo – Lake Pepin in foreground, Point-no-Point in background on
    right, from the Bay City community park, 63
Photo – Mom, 1968, 130
Photo – Red Wing Mn. Mississippi River Bridge from Minnesota shore,
    Wisconsin in background *c.* 1920, 61
Photo – Regent, ND – Dad, 1945, 129
Photo – Regent, ND – Dad, 1949, 129
Photo – Tabor Church, rural Bay City. Taken in 1980s, 136
Photo – Wedding pictures: Earnest A. Reitan, Caren Helene Reitan, 23
Point-no-Point, 42, 63, 64, 123
Prohibition, 10, 31, 43, 94
Puritanical, 31

R

radio, 29, 31, 59, 66, 81, 91, 92, 95, 96, 123
Red Wing, 42, 43, 50, 51, 56, 59, 61, 68
Redin, Ella, 36
Reed, Jimmy, 49, 123
Regent, ND, 100
Reitan Gaarden, 4
Reitan, Aunt Beatrice (Mrs. Maurice Nelson), 17, 21, 24
Reitan, Aunt Florence (Gust), 21
Reitan, Aunt Lou (Mrs. Dr. Meudeking), 15 - 17, 132
Reitan, Aunt Rose (Mrs. Ben Samstad), 10, 14, 15, 18, 19, 22, 32, 57, 62,
    99, 129, 130, 132
Reitan, C. C., 4, 8, 9, 10, 13
Reitan, Carl, 21, 25, 29, 91
Reitan, Carol, 19
Reitan, Clayton, 41, 47, 57, 60, 69, 75, 78, 79, 131, 135
Reitan, Conrad, 9, 13, 14, 15, 18, 19, 22
Reitan, Gust, 20, 21, 27, 36, 62
Reitan, Henry, 112
Reitan, Julia, 37
Reitan, Ludovic, 4, 9
Reitan, Norma, 19, 72, 73, 89, 94, 96, 131
Reitan, Ole C., 9
Reitan, Phil, 41, 44, 45, 47, 57, 60, 69, 79, 85, 131, 135
Reitan, Reuben, 13, 19, 20, 22, 23, 32
robbery at Bay City Stat Bank, 61
Roberts, Clark, 69

Rosendale, 27, 30, 36

S

Samstad, Uncle Ben, 18
Sauk Centre, Mn., 89
Schultz, Julene, 68
Schultz's Store, 66
Selective Service System, 96
Sioux Falls, 18
Spriggle, Fritz, 54
St. Olaf Choir, 106
St. Olaf College, 103
Starbuck, Mn., 86
Statue of Liberty, 12
Stevens County, 67
Stevens County Historical Society, 135
Stroud, 36
Swanson, Sgt. Earl, 120

T

tap team, 82
Terry, 49, 50, 123
Thompson, Sigvald, 106
Treischel's cafe, 65
Trinity Lutheran Church, 83, 109, 131
Trondheim, 3, 4, 7
tuberculosis, 30
Twin Cities, 7, 15, 35, 46

V

Velva, ND, 25
Venberg, Irving - violin teacher, 58
Voltaire, ND, 25

W

Weeks, Rev. Earl, 38
Welk, Lawrence, 92
Wilde, Ran, 82
Williston, ND, 28
Willmar, 16, 17, 24, 42, 87
Willmar Seminary, 24
Winona, 16
Women's Christian Temperance Union, 10
World War II, 20, 30, 79, 92, 134

Wyman, Mark, 135

Y

Yon Yonson, 51

Z

Zephyr, 46